P · O · C · K · E · T · S

CATS

OCELOT

IVORY PANEL
(8TH CENTURY B.C.)
OF A MAN-EATING LION

BLUE ABYSSINIAN

P · O · C · K · E · T · S
CATS

Written by
DAVID ALDERTON

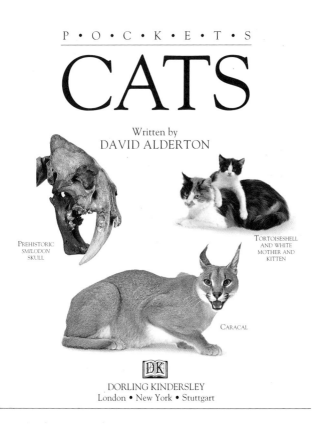

PREHISTORIC
SMILODON
SKULL

TORTOISESHELL
AND WHITE
MOTHER AND
KITTEN

CARACAL

DK

DORLING KINDERSLEY
London • New York • Stuttgart

A DORLING KINDERSLEY BOOK

Project editor Elise Bradbury
Art editor Clair Watson
Senior editor Laura Buller
Senior art editor Helen Senior
Production Louise Barratt
Catherine Semark
Picture research Fiona Watson

First published in Great Britain in 1995
by Dorling Kindersley Limited
9 Henrietta Street, Covent Garden, London WC2E 8PS

4 6 8 10 9 7 5 3

Visit us on the World Wide Web at http://www.dk.com

A CIP catalogue record for this book is available from
the British Library.

ISBN 0 7513 5181 4

Colour reproduction by Colourscan, Singapore
Printed and bound in Italy by L.E.G.O.

CONTENTS

How to use this book

These pages show you how to use *Pockets: Cats*. The book is divided into several sections. The main section consists of information about different breeds of domestic cats as well as many of the wild cats. There is also an introductory section at the front of the book, and a reference section at the back. Each new section begins with a page that lists what will follow in that section.

Different types of cats

The domestic cats in this book are divided into groups according to coat length. The wild cats have their own separate section. Within each section, there is detailed information about different species or breeds.

Corner coding

The top corners of the pages in a section are colour coded to remind you which section you are in.

	SIMILAR CATS WITH DIFFERENT COATS
	LONGHAIRED CATS
	SHORTHAIRED CATS
	THE WORLD'S WILD CATS

Corner coding

Heading

Introduction

Caption

SIMILAR CATS WITH DIFFERENT COATS

ABYSSINIAN AND SOMALI

THE FIRST ABYSSINIAN CATS were brought to Britain in 1868 by soldiers returning from war in Abyssinia (now Ethiopia). Abyssinians look so similar to the cats in ancient Egyptian wallpaintings that they are believed to be related. The Somali breed originated from long-coated kittens in Abyssinian litters.

BLUE ABYSSINIAN

Ticked fur is short, thick, and glossy

RUDDY ABYSSINIAN

TRADITIONAL COLOURING

The original Abyssinian is known as the Usual or Ruddy. It is sometimes called the "rabbit cat" because the orangish brown ticked colour of its coat is like a wild rabbit's. These athletic and lively cats have been popular pets for decades.

TWO-TONE COAT

The Blue Abyssinian used to be quite rare, but is now becoming more common. It has a steel blue-grey coat with an oatmeal-coloured undercoat. New colours are developed by cross-breeding with other types of cat.

52

Heading

The heading describes the subject of the page. This page is about the Abyssinian and Somali pedigree cat breeds.

Introduction

This provides a clear, general overview of the subject. After reading this, you should have an idea what the pages are about.

Captions and annotations

Each illustration has a caption. Annotations, in *italics*, point out features of an illustration and usually have leader lines.

RUNNING HEADS

These remind you which section you are in. The top of the left-hand page gives the section name. The right-hand page gives the subject. This page on the Abyssinian and Somali breeds is in the Similar Cats with Different Coats section.

FEATURE BOXES

Throughout the book, feature boxes supply extra information. This feature box gives details about the fur colour of Abyssinians and Somalis.

FACT BOXES

Many pages have fact boxes. These contain at-a-glance, interesting information about the topic. Fact boxes include specific information about the subject matter that is discussed on the page.

Running head   *Feature box*

Label   *Annotation*

REFERENCE SECTION

The reference section pages are yellow and are found at the back of the book. On these, you will find useful facts and practical tips. These pages give you information on choosing and caring for a cat, as well as amazing cat records.

LABELS

For extra clarity, many of the pictures have labels. These may give extra information, or identify a picture when it is not obvious from the text.

INDEX

You will find an index at the back of this book. This lists alphabetically every subject and every type of cat that is covered in the rest of the book.

INTRODUCTION TO CATS

WHAT IS A CAT?

CATS ARE NATURE'S most efficiently designed hunting carnivores. They have powerful bodies, superb vision, and razor-sharp teeth and claws. Most cats are self-reliant, stalking their prey alone in dusk or darkness. One species has also succeeded in living with people, and is now kept as a pet around the world.

AFRICAN LION

ANCIENT EGYPTIAN CAT

Short, rounded head

Sandy-brown coat for camouflage

Cats lived near settlements, where they could easily find food.

Strong front legs and muscular neck for catching prey

Sharp claws are kept sheathed when not in use

HISTORY OF THE DOMESTIC CAT
Wall paintings show that cats were being tamed in ancient Egypt before 2500 B.C. Although the Egyptians forbade the export of their cats, they still spread to ancient Greece by 500 B.C. They were also recorded in India before 100 B.C.

MOTHER AND KITTEN

TYPICAL MAMMAL

Like other mammals, cats are warm-blooded and have a skeleton and a four-chambered heart. The female gives birth to live young and produces milk to feed her kittens.

Loose skin for freedom of movement

Flexible backbone increases length of stride as cat runs

Tail is one-third the length of the body

Back legs are powered by the largest muscles in the cat's body

THE HUNTER

Virtually everything about a cat, including the domestic cat, is designed for hunting. Cats are lithe, intelligent, and strong, and react with lightning speed. A cat approaches its prey using stealth and camouflage, then overpowers its victim. Lions are the only cats that hunt in groups.

Long, dark hair at tip of tail is used for signalling

THE FIRST CATS

A SMALL CARNIVORE similar to a pine marten hunted
in the trees of prehistoric forests 50 million years ago.
This was the cat's most distant
ancestor. Some 12 million
years ago, the first true
cats evolved. Many
of these first
types of cat
no longer
exist.

*Large crest held
powerful muscles
that were used to
snap the jaws
closed*

SMILODON SKULL
FROM 15,000
YEARS AGO

*Weak lower jaw; most
of the force came from
the top jaw*

*Large
teeth for
ripping*

*Canine teeth
6 in (15 cm)
long protruded
from sides of
mouth when jaw
was shut*

DEADLY FANGS
Smilodon is the best-known
of the prehistoric sabre-
toothed cats. Until 15,000
years ago these cats roamed
the grasslands in groups, like
modern-day lions. They preyed
on huge, slow-moving
herbivores such as mammoths
and camels, using their dagger-like
teeth to stab their ponderous victims.

SABRE-TOOTH
KILL

Mammoth struggling in sticky tar

RANCHO LA BREA TAR PIT
The remains of over 2,000 *Smilodon*
cats have been found in this U.S. site.
Over centuries, sabre-tooths came
here to prey on animals trapped in tar
and then became stuck themselves.

WHERE THEY LIVED
Smilodon lived mainly in North
America. Similar cats known as
Megantereon ranged across northern
India, Africa, and the Mediterranean
coast, as well as North America.
More recently, lions and giant
cheetahs roamed Europe.

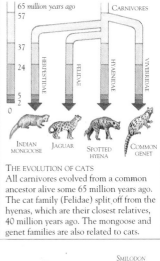

65 million years ago			CARNIVORES
57			
37			
24			
5			
2			
0			

HERPESTIDAE   FELIDAE   HYAENIDAE   VIVERRIDAE

INDIAN MONGOOSE   JAGUAR   SPOTTED HYENA   COMMON GENET

THE EVOLUTION OF CATS
All carnivores evolved from a common
ancestor alive some 65 million years ago.
The cat family (Felidae) split off from the
hyenas, which are their closest relatives,
40 million years ago. The mongoose and
genet families are also related to cats.

SMILODON
RECONSTRUCTION
FROM FOSSIL
REMAINS

*Smilodon was
about the same size
as a modern lion.*

*Exact colour is
unknown*

TYPES OF CAT

THE CAT FAMILY includes about 39 species of cat, from the tiger to the domestic cat. Depending on whether they live in the desert, savannah, forest, jungle – or in our homes – the different types of cat vary widely in size, colour, markings, and way of life.

MOUNTAIN DWELLER
The adaptable bobcat lives in a wide range of North American habitats, from swamps to snowy mountains. Bobcats are one of only two types of wild cat with short, stumpy tails. They are still hunted for their fur.

DOMESTIC CATS
One of the smallest members of the cat family, the domestic cat is found nearly everywhere. These cats still sometimes interbreed with their ancestors, the wild cats.

Massive paws can strike a fatal blow

RED POINT
BRITISH
SHORTHAIR

INDIAN
TIGER

CLIMBING CATS
Some types of cat specialize in climbing. Leopards are the biggest of these excellent climbers. They will scale a tree and then ambush unsuspecting animals that pass underneath. Some small cats regularly hunt birds and lizards in the leafy treetops of the forest.

UNIQUE GRASSLANDS HUNTER
The cheetah is classed in a distinct group from all the other cats because it is best at running rather than leaping. Its unrivalled speed and acute vision have evolved for hunting in open country.

LEOPARD

Leopards are found in Asia and Africa.

BIG CAT
The tiger is the largest and most powerful of all the cats. Tigers can live from the rainforests of Southeast Asia to the harsh cold of Siberia. Siberian tigers are the biggest of the group. Tigers cannot run quickly for long, but are strong enough to tackle large prey. They are also fine swimmers.

The Indian tiger can weigh up to 260 kg (573 lb).

Unique striped pattern camouflages the animal in forests

CAT ANATOMY

ALL CATS ARE AGILE and athletic predators. Their
bodies are powerful and flexible, specially designed
for running, jumping, and climbing. Some types of cat
even excel at swimming. Superb hunters, cats first
swiftly chase and then overpower prey with
their strength. Sharp teeth
are used to finish
off the catch.

Tail provides
balance

Muscular
back legs
propel cat
forwards

Number of
bones in tail
varies in
different
species

POWER LEAP
Strong hind legs provide thrust so
the cat can pounce on prey. Sure-footed,
it lands safely even on slippery surfaces.

Body elongates
(becomes long and
thin) as cat stretches
out to leap

Neck vertebrae

Deep
rib cage

Front legs are
shorter than
hind legs

BARE BONES
A cat's skeleton has about
250 bones. The seven vertebrae in
the neck are shorter than in most other
mammals, and the spine is very flexible.
This is a domestic cat skeleton, but the
skeletons of the larger cats are similar.

Liver
Oesophagus
Stomach
Anus
Bladder
Small intestine
Heart
Diaphragm

INTERNAL ORGANS

The intestines of a cat are short and simple since they need to digest only meat and not plants. Most of the nutrients from the food are absorbed in the small intestine.

Powerful jaw muscles attach to side of skull

Incisor, or biting, teeth

Canine teeth to kill prey

Carnassial teeth to tear prey apart

Front legs take most of the impact of landing

Pads on the feet help cushion the cat as it lands

CAT SKULL

A cat's skull is large compared to the size of its body. The eye sockets are big to allow for good range of vision. The jaws are short and strong. All of a cat's teeth are sharp and scissor-like for tearing and cutting, rather than flat, like a human's, for crushing.

Heads and faces

With its powerful eyesight, acute hearing, strong jaws, and sharp teeth, a cat's head is designed for efficiently killing prey. To be an effective hunter, a cat must be able to think quickly, so cats have quite large brains. Domestic cats share these qualities with their wild relatives. However, selective breeding (when cats are specially bred by humans to develop particular characteristics) has created a huge variety of head shapes and facial features. Cats' faces may also change as they age.

HISTORICAL SIAMESE
A breed's appearance can change over time. This prize-winning Siamese from the early 1900s has a rounded face far removed from today's Siamese cats.

Adult tom cats develop jowls that look like a double chin.

Nose is pug-like, sometimes causing breathing difficulties

Siamese cats have large, pointed ears with wide bases.

ROUND FACE
It is often possible to identify a domestic breed by its face shape. The British Shorthair has a distinctly rounded face and large head. Its ears are set wide apart.

FLAT FACE
The facial shape of the Persian, the oldest of the longhaired breeds, has changed dramatically over the last hundred years. Today Persians have extremely flat faces.

WEDGE FACE
A triangular face is now typical of Siamese and Oriental cats. In cat shows, a Siamese is judged by its slender, angular head and its almond-shaped eyes.

THE KING OF THE BEASTS
A lion has the most recognizable head of any type
of cat. The unique mane of the male lion makes it
the only member of the cat family that can
easily be distinguished from the female
of the same species. The purpose
of the lion's mane is probably
to make him look more
threatening. Only mature
males are able to grow a
mane – neutered
males cannot.

*The colour and size of
the mane vary
between individuals.*

AFRICAN
LION

*Male lions roar as part
of their challenge to
other males.*

*The broad
muzzle gives
power to the
lion's jaws.*

HEAD &
FACE FACTS

• Cheetahs
have longer noses
than other cats.
This helps them to
breathe more easily
when holding prey.

• Each individual
tiger has distinctive
head markings.

• A cat born with
four ears was recorded
in the U.S.A. in 1978.

Eyes and ears

As predators, cats depend on their highly developed senses of sight and hearing to find prey. The majority of cats hunt at night, so they need to be able to see in near darkness. A cat can see about six times better than a person can at night. However, a cat's colour vision is not as developed as ours. Cats also rely on their acute hearing to pinpoint the exact location of prey. Sounds inaudible to humans, or even dogs, can be detected by cats.

SOUND DETECTORS
The serval, a cat from the African savannah, has large, mobile ears. It can pick up the high-pitched calls of rodents hidden in the grass.

THE OUTER EAR
A cat's outer ear acts like a funnel, channelling sounds to the eardrum. Each ear can rotate to locate sounds precisely.

Ossicles (ear bones) send sound into inner ear

Semi-circular canals filled with fluid

Cochlea changes vibrations into nerve impulses

Auditory nerve takes signals to brain

THE INNER EAR
Sound waves vibrate the eardrum, which then moves the ossicles. The vibrations change to electrical impulses and travel down the auditory nerve to the brain. Here they are deciphered into meaningful sounds.

Ear-drum picks up sound waves

Oval window takes sound waves to cochlea

2 2

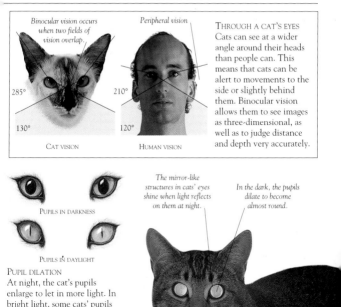

Binocular vision occurs when two fields of vision overlap.

Peripheral vision

285°

130°

210°

120°

CAT VISION

HUMAN VISION

THROUGH A CAT'S EYES
Cats can see at a wider
angle around their heads
than people can. This
means that cats can be
alert to movements to the
side or slightly behind
them. Binocular vision
allows them to see images
as three-dimensional, as
well as to judge distance
and depth very accurately.

PUPILS IN DARKNESS

PUPILS IN DAYLIGHT

PUPIL DILATION
At night, the cat's pupils
enlarge to let in more light. In
bright light, some cats' pupils
narrow to slits; others contract
to small circles.

SEEING IN THE DARK
Cats see well in semi-darkness.
This is because of a "mirror" of
glittering cells (called the
tapetum lucidum) behind
the retina. These cells
reflect light back, making
objects clearer in the dark.

*The mirror-like
structures in cats' eyes
shine when light reflects
on them at night.*

*In the dark, the pupils
dilate to become
almost round.*

Smell, taste, and touch

Cats have extremely acute senses. They rely on smell to
identify the things around them, and on touch to feel their
way around, particularly in the dark. Another sensory
device cats possess is the Jacobsen's organ, located
in the roof of the mouth. This structure seems
to respond to both smell and taste, and helps
the cat to detect scents that their
nose cannot – for example,
when a female is
ready to mate.

*Cats never eat
anything without
carefully sniffing it first.*

*The senses of
smell and taste
tell the cat if
this toad is
edible.*

SENSE OF SMELL
A cat's nose contains some
19 million smelling nerves, compared to
a human's 5 million. Cats are especially
sensitive to rancid odours, such as meat
that has gone off. They normally seek
out fresh meat rather than scavenge
dead animals.

ENTICING CATNIP
Many cats, especially tom (male)
cats, find the smell of catnip
irresistible. This garden herb
contains a chemical that
relaxes cats, or can make them
roll around. About 50 per cent of
cats do not react to catnip at all.

TOUCH-SENSITIVE HAIRS

Whiskers are specialized, stiff hairs with highly sensitive nerves in their roots. They help a cat like this leopard to familiarize itself with its surroundings. A cat uses its whiskers to gauge if it can fit through a gap.

The cat's saliva leaves its scent.

Cats groom each other to spread their scent, and also to show affection.

CAT COMMUNICATION

Cats use smell to communicate far more than people do. They recognize the familiar scents of their companions. Because their skin is covered in touch-sensitive nerves, cats also communicate by grooming each other.

Characteristic lip-curling known as flehmening

FLEHMENING

The curious way that a cat curls its upper lip is called flehmening. It does this to draw smells into the Jacobsen's organ in its mouth. Male cats flehmen to detect the scent of nearby females. The Jacobsen's organs of the lion and tiger are more sensitive than those of domestic cats.

Paws and claws

A cat uses its paws for everything from gentle grooming to fierce fighting. To aid a cat in one of its most important skills, running, the bones of the feet have evolved so that a cat permanently walks on its toes. In the wild, injuries to the paws can prove fatal, as these can prevent a cat from hunting successfully.

CLAWS FOR CLIMBING

Most cats are masterly climbers, and can make even a vertical ascent with ease. Coming back down is more problematic, since the claws curve the wrong way to grip when descending. Cats awkwardly make their way down a tree backwards.

Claws are made of keratin, like human nails.

Dew claw on front leg is placed like a thumb and helps to grip

Claws dig in to anchor the cat

Carpal pad on front paw prevents skidding when cat lands

SPECIALIZED FEET

A cat has furless pads of tough leather on the underside of its paws. These pads enable the animal to stalk silently, and they cushion the impact of landings. Pads also help the cat to "brake" suddenly in mid-run. The cheetah has unique grooved pads to improve its control when running.

SCRATCHING ITS MARK
This jaguar, like other cats, scratches trees to keep its claws clean and sharp. Scratching also marks a cat's territory. A cat leaves behind its scent from glands between its toes, while the scratches themselves show the cat has been in the area.

HUNTING WEAPONS
Watching a cat play will reveal many of its hunting techniques. Cats use their front paws to swipe at, scoop up, rake, or grip their catch. Playing with toys is one way domestic cats practise these moves. Pets tend not to use their claws ferociously against their owners.

Claws extended to grasp toy

This 3-week-old kitten is already beginning to develop its hunting skills.

RETRACTABLE CLAWS
When a cat rests, ligaments keep its claws protected under extensions of the toe bones. The claws are only extended when needed. A cheetah, however, has its claws out permanently so it can grip the ground when it runs.

CLAWS RETRACTED

CLAWS EXTENDED

Relaxed cat with claws retracted out of sight

Ligaments slacken to unveil claws when necessary

FUR TYPES

SLEEK AND FINE, or long and luxurious, a cat's fur is its finest feature. The coat insulates a cat in hot or cold weather, carries its scent, and is sensitive to touch. Fur type is often suited to where a cat lives, although the wide variation of coats in domestic breeds is due to selective breeding by people.

Awn hairs

Down hairs *Guard hairs*

A CAT'S COAT
There are three kinds of hair in a cat's coat, although not every breed has all three. The longest are the coarse outer guard hairs. In wild and domestic cats, these carry the fur pattern. Slightly shorter awn hairs lie beneath. Short, soft down provides insulation.

Persians have thick down and up to 10-cm (4-in) long guard hairs.

BRITISH SHORTHAIR
This breed is typical of short-coated cats. It has a short, dense, crisp coat. The thick, plush fur stands out from the body like a rug.

Coat is about 5 cm (2 in) thick

PERSIAN LONGHAIR
Persian cats have the longest and densest fur of any cat breed. The hairs are silky and fine, giving the cat a very fluffy appearance – even the paws are tufted. In warm summer months the cat moults, which makes its coat look shorter.

Fur is especially curly on back and tail

AMERICAN WIREHAIR

This cat's fur is distinctively wiry and springy. Every hair, including those in the ears and on the tail, is crimped, or even coiled. The Wirehair's fur is of medium length and very frizzy. It feels like lamb's-wool to the touch.

Wiry coat makes pattern look raised

CORNISH REX

The unusual fur of the Rex breeds is wavy and crimped. All of the hairs in a Cornish Rex's coat are short and curly. The coat is made up solely of down and awn hairs, both of which are very soft to the touch. The fur is fine, so Rexes can be susceptible to the cold.

WILD CAT FUR

Wild cats have coats of two layers: warm down hair underneath and a resilient outer coat. In cold climates, cats have thicker fur. The Pallas's cat from Asia has the longest coat of any wild cat. It was once mistakenly believed to be the ancestor of domestic cats with long hair.

Longer fur on underside for warmth when lying on cold ground

PALLAS'S CAT

"HAIRLESS" SPHYNX

Although the Sphynx looks bald, it has traces of fur on its tail and a light covering of down on its body. It also has very short eyebrows and whiskers. This breed's lack of hair means that it is vulnerable to sunburn.

Coat is like suede

Colours and patterns

Cats come in a huge variety of colours and patterns.
Many have distinctive markings that originally
evolved to help cats in the wild stay hidden
from their prey. Domestic cats often come in
more conspicuous colours because they
have little need for camouflage.
Breeders have achieved
some very striking colour
and pattern combinations.

SEAL TORTIE
POINT SIAMESE

CORNISH REX
TORTOISESHELL

HIMALAYAN POINTS
Siamese cats have a characteristic pattern of
darker areas on the tail, legs, ears, and face.
These markings are described as points. Young
kittens develop their points as they mature.

*Black and red
randomly but
evenly distributed*

WHITE

TORTOISESHELL
For genetic
reasons, tortoiseshell patterns
occur almost entirely in female
cats. Tortoiseshell fur is a
combination of black and red.

RED

BLACK

CHOCOLATE

COLOUR RANGE
Some cats have unpatterned coats
of one pure, solid colour. There are
many varieties, some simply paler
versions of the basic colours. Here
the typical darker colours are shown
above their lighter variants, with
white shown on its own.

CREAM

BLUE

LILAC

TABBY MARKINGS

This cat's spotted coat exemplifies the dark markings typical of tabbies. In different tabby cats, the patterning might be stripes, spots, or patches. These patterns are left over from the natural camouflage markings of wild cats. Tabby patterning is very common in feral cats (domestic cats that live in the wild).

SILVER SPOTTED BRITISH SHORTHAIR

Black spots are striking against a silver background

WILD CAT PATTERNS

The stripes or spots of a wild cat's coat are vital because they help the animal blend into its surroundings. Patterns camouflage a cat by breaking up the outline of its body shape. The markings of wild cats vary so considerably that the shape of the patterns is one way to distinguish the species. Individual cats of the same species also have slightly varying patterns.

Each individual ocelot has a different pattern.

Golden coat with black markings

OCELOT

Markings break up cat's outline in forests

Bold, ringed black spots

JAGUAR

Unique striped markings

Named after its cloud-like pattern

Grey-brown coat with marbled markings

TIGER

CLOUDED LEOPARD

CAT MOVEMENT

NORMALLY GRACEFUL and controlled, cats can also react with a sudden burst of energy. Balance, strength, speed, and quick judgement help cats to chase and seize elusive prey. The only physical quality cats lack is endurance. The cat is a particularly talented leaper, able to jump four and a half times its body length and land on a chosen spot with great accuracy.

JUMPING

Cats can leap vertically when necessary. The caracal and lynx are expert jumpers, leaping up into the air to swipe a bird as it takes off. With one paw, they can knock their catch to the ground.

A kitten extends its paws and claws to prepare for landing.

Head outstretched as cheetah accelerates to its full speed

CHEETAH

TERRITORIAL MOVEMENTS

One of a cat's main daily movements is to patrol and mark its territory. It will roam around looking out for other cats or potential prey. Cats climb both to survey their area and because a higher position gives them an advantage over competitors.

Claws help a cat climb and maintain its balance.

Looking before leaping, to judge its distance from the ground

LEAPING

A cat's most characteristic movement is its leap, demonstrated here by a lioness. The back muscles flex and relax as the cat leaps, with the tail extended for balance. The powerful back legs lift the cat and are the last part of the body to leave the ground.

The lioness stretches her body forwards as she takes off.

Tail is turned up for balance

Slender, light body and long legs enable the cheetah to reach high speeds

The tail is more than half the length of the body. It swings to counterbalance the body during sharp turns.

RUNNING

Most cats can leap better than they run, but the cheetah is built for speed. Its backbone is extremely flexible, so when the front legs touch the ground, the back end springs forwards. In mid-stride the body stretches full out and all four legs leave the ground. At full sprint the cheetah can reach 96 km/h (60 mph).

When running, the front paws never touch the ground at the same time as the back paws.

Balancing and falling

Some types of cat spend a significant part of their lives in trees, moving confidently along even the narrowest branches. However, if it does fall, the cat has evolved a unique method of protecting itself. Its eyes, brain, and sensitive balance organs in the inner ear ensure that the cat always lands on its feet.

The head rotates first to align with the ground.

1 INSTANT REACTION
The inner ear instantly reacts if the cat is off balance. This warns the brain that it needs to begin to respond to the fall.

2 ROTATING RAPIDLY
The front of the body receives signals from the brain and twists to follow the head. The backbone is so supple that it can rotate 180°.

Front legs pull around to upright position

GEOFFROY'S CAT

LIVING THE HIGH LIFE
Many of the small wild cats hunt and sleep in trees. The Geoffroy's cat from South America uses its sharp claws, keen eyesight, good reflexes, and superb sense of balance to stalk mammals and birds in the treetops.

This cat lives in the mountainous forests of southern South America.

PERFECT BALANCE

This leopard looks precariously balanced, but it will easily secure its kill off the ground and away from scavengers. The leopard is one of the biggest members of the cat family that spends a lot of time in the trees. It is strong enough to drag up a carcass heavier than its own body weight.

FALLING FACTS

• One cat is known to have survived a record fall of 61 m (200 ft).

• From heights of 18 m (60 ft), cats travel at 64 km/h (40 mph) before they hit the ground.

• If the front legs cannot absorb the force of impact, the cat's chin crashes into the ground. This is likely to cause a jaw fracture.

Back end still recovering

Eyes checking where it will be landing

The back legs will help to absorb the force of impact.

4 LANDING ON ITS FEET
Only seconds after losing its balance, the cat is well positioned to land safely. The head and soft underparts are protected from injury. The cat instinctively relaxes its body before impact, which prevents it from tearing its muscles or jarring its joints.

3 READY FOR IMPACT
As the cat's front legs begin to stretch out to make contact with the ground, the back of the body is still swivelling around. The collarbones at the top of the front legs will act as shock absorbers when the cat lands.

Legs prepared to run when cat touches ground

Front legs take most of the shock of the landing

LIFE CYCLE OF CATS

A HEALTHY CAT can live for 10–20 years. Before they are a year old, cats of small species begin to breed. The big cats do not have their first litter until at least the age of three. Female cats have evolved an unusual but efficient breeding cycle. Mating triggers the release of the eggs, increasing the cat's chance of getting pregnant.

LIONS COURTING
A lion grooms his partner before mating. He will try to prevent any other males from coming near. A pair may mate 100 times in a day.

Finding a partner

Several times a year, when she is ready to mate ("on heat"), a female cat (or queen) calls loudly to allure a partner. Her urine contains chemical scents known as *pheromones*. These waft through the air, attracting potential mates in the area. She can then select one or more candidates to father her kittens.

Tom eyes queen

1 THE FIRST MEETING
The queen is unlikely to accept a mate straight away. She may even react aggressively at first, before becoming provocative and enticing the tom by rolling on the ground.

Rolling is a typical signal that a queen is on heat.

2 RITUAL REJECTION

The tom cat approaches to make initial contact, but the queen drives off any attempt to mate until she is ready. She will lunge out with her claws or bite to free herself if necessary. He will repeat his advance moments later.

Male tries to grab neck to prevent her attack

Female spurns the tom's first approach

Mating lasts only a few seconds.

Eggs may be released 24 hours after mating

3 MATING

When she is ready to mate, the female raises her hindquarters and puts her tail to one side. The male stops her from turning on him by gripping the loose skin, or scruff, of her neck.

4 AFTER THE ACT

Once they have separated, both cats groom themselves. Cats usually mate repeatedly over a few days. Often the female mates with several toms. As a result, one litter can contain kittens with different fathers.

The male rests for awhile.

The female may not have anything to do with the male after mating.

Growing up

It takes kittens about 65 days to develop in the womb. The pregnancy of big wild cats lasts for 115 days. Once born, all young cats are helpless. They are blind and deaf for over a week and must huddle together for warmth. Kittens grow quickly and are independent by three months, but cubs in the wild can stay with their mother for up to two years.

Average litter size is four, but some cats have much larger litters

BEFORE BIRTH

A kitten's organs develop in its first weeks in the uterus. Only in the last three weeks do the foetuses grow much in size. This prevents the mother from being hindered by a weight increase, so she can hunt until late in pregnancy.

These kittens are in their last weeks before birth.

Each foetus develops inside a sac-like membrane.

FAMILY FACTS

• One Burmese had a record 19 kittens in a single litter.

• All kittens have blue eyes. As they grow up their eyes often change colour.

• Cats can breed throughout life; one female had a kitten when she was 28.

FIRST FEEDING

A mother cat must bring up her young on her own. She suckles her kittens for six to eight weeks. Although she has only eight teats, she can rear up to 14 kittens.

The first milk has antibodies to help kittens fight infections.

STARTING ON SOLID FOOD
Young cubs in the wild may not eat meat until
three months old, while kittens are
weaned in about half that time. The
mother still protects her young after
they stop suckling. She also
teaches them cleaning
and hunting skills.

*As the cat grows up, the
colour or pattern of its
coat may change slightly.*

*A kitten's fur is
downy soft until it
grows its adult
guard hairs.*

CHEETAH
AND CUBS

A MOTHER'S CARE
Having to look after her cubs alone makes
life difficult for a female cheetah. She is
forced to leave her young while she
hunts, and goes to great lengths to
protect them. From the time they
are born until they are old
enough to follow her, she
may carry them one by one
to up to 20 new
locations. She must
keep them hidden
from predators
like lions and
leopards.

*Nine out of ten
cheetah cubs do
not survive their
first three
months.*

*In its first year, a
young cheetah has
a mane of longer
hair on its neck.*

HUNTING

VIRTUALLY ALL CATS hunt on their
own, so they must attack
with surprise and speed.
They stealthily approach
their unsuspecting prey
using any available cover.
When they are close enough
they suddenly pounce, seizing
their quarry in a deadly grip.

HOUSEHOLD HUNTER
The domestic cat is famed for
its prowess as a mouser. Some cats
also excel at catching lizards, birds,
or insects. However, hunting is a
learned behaviour, so not all pet
cats make efficient hunters.

GROUP CHASE
Unlike most cats, lions hunt
in groups. This means they
can kill animals larger than
themselves. The lionesses of
the pride do nearly all of
the hunting. To improve
their chances of a kill,
they single out a weak-
looking animal,
surround it, and then
chase it down.

*Cat holds its body
and tail close to
the ground*

FATAL BITE
This leopard pins down its victim to stop it from escaping. Then it bites through the neck of its catch to sever the spinal cord. If a cat cannot eat its kill all at once it will drag the carcass under cover to protect it from scavengers.

FRUSTRATED KILLER
Domestic cats will play with a toy as if it were a prey animal. They creep up on the object, then bite and shake it. Wild cats sometimes toy with their quarry before killing it.

Spotted coat pattern keeps the animal camouflaged

Mature cats play occasionally, but not as often as kittens.

ASIAN
LEOPARD CAT

SILENT STALKER
Except for the cheetah, cats can manage only short bursts of speed. They must steal quite close to an animal before they bound forwards. Approaching slowly and silently, the stalking cat is alert to every movement. When it is within striking distance it springs on its prey without warning.

The cat runs forwards in this position, then stops and crouches down.

GROOMING

BOTH WILD AND DOMESTIC cats are extremely clean creatures. Meticulous, regular grooming keeps a cat's coat glossy and healthy by getting rid of dirt, loose hair, and dead skin. Grooming also allows a cat to spread its scent all around its body. Usually grooming is the sign of a relaxed cat, but sometimes it can be a nervous reaction.

WASHING EACH OTHER

A cat may need help cleaning areas it cannot quite reach. Mutual grooming also reinforces the bond between family members, like these kittens, as they spread their scent over each other.

The paws must be kept free of irritating thorns and grit.

Each papilla points backwards, so tongue can be used like a rasp

GROOMING TOOL

The cat's tongue is rough, covered in pointed, abrasive hooks called *papillae*. These enable the tongue to be used like a comb when pulled through fur. *Papillae* are also tough enough to scrape meat off a bone.

Tongue curls like a ladle to lap up liquid

CLEANING UP

Like domestic cats, wild cats such as this snow leopard often groom themselves when they have finished feeding. This removes the blood from their fur after a kill. Grooming may also help a cat cool off in hot weather as the saliva evaporates from its coat.

Flexible body means the cat can bend to lick almost all areas of its body

Scent from glands on the chin, paws, and near the genitals is spread all over the coat.

GROOMING FACTS

• Cats always groom themselves after waking from a deep sleep.

• The hair swallowed during grooming can form a furball in the cat's stomach.

• The largest recorded furball weighed 57 g (2 oz). It was surgically removed from a 14-year-old cat.

WASHING ROUTINE
Every time it cleans itself, a cat follows exactly the same routine. It licks its paw and wipes it in circles around the sides of the face and the ears.

SIMILAR CATS WITH DIFFERENT COATS

ABOUT DIFFERENT COAT LENGTHS

CATS' COATS COME in a wide variety of different lengths and textures. Sometimes these variations have evolved naturally or are the result of chance matings between cats. This section focuses on particular breeds with close relatives that have been purposely bred to achieve a different type of coat.

Distinct ruff of fur around neck

Bushy tail

SILKY TIFFANIE
This long-coated counterpart of the Burmese was developed in the 1970s from a desire to create a Burmese with a fluffy coat. The Tiffanie is not as popular as its sleek relative. This may be because its long fur conceals the elegant body shape.

BURMESE
A distant descendant of Southeast Asian cats dating back to the 15th century, the Burmese has a fine, short coat, well suited to the heat and humidity of the tropics.

TURN-OF-THE-CENTURY PERSIAN

For the last 100 years, people have specially bred cats to emphasize certain features, including coat length. Comparing this Persian Longhair from the 1900s to its descendant below shows how, over time, the coat has become longer and fluffier.

Breeders have enhanced the long, luxurious coat.

MODERN PERSIAN

This tortie and white Persian is a top example of its kind today. Its undercoat is so thick that it makes the cat appear much larger than its actual size.

Today Persians come in a huge range of colours.

BRITISH SHORTHAIR

PERSIAN LONGHAIR

COAT COMPARISON

The length of a cat's coat does not affect its colour. However, tabby markings are more distinct on shorthaired cats because their hair is compact. In longhaired cats, the down hair determines how dense the coat is.

AMERICAN CURL

THESE UNUSUAL-LOOKING CATS are a recent breed, originating in 1981. American Curls are so-named because their ears curl backwards, appearing almost inside out. This chance mutation was noticed by two breeders in California, U.S.A., and has since been developed in both longhaired and shorthaired versions. These cats do not seem to suffer as a result of their curled ears.

LONGHAIRED CURL
The first American Curl was a longhaired female kitten whose ear cartilage began to curve backwards a few days after she was born. She passed on this odd trait to two of her kittens.

Silky coat and plumed tail

Cats with curled ears can be bred in any colour or pattern.

RED TABBY AND WHITE AMERICAN CURL

*Ears can swivel so
tips point inwards*

*Soft, rounded
ear tips*

TABBY TORTIE AND WHITE
AMERICAN CURL

CURLED EARS
Instead of rising to a point, the
American Curl's ears curve backwards
to at least a 90° angle. The degree that
the ears curl depends on the
individual cat.

*The base of
the ears is
quite firm.*

*Round face
with straight
nose*

SHORTHAIRED CURL
This fur type was achieved by
crossing shorthaired cats with
the original longhaired
American Curls. It takes four
to seven days for a newborn
kitten's ears to begin to curl.
The ears continue
to unfurl for months.
Breeders prefer an
extreme curl.

*Crossing American Curls with
Siamese cats has introduced
coloured points.*

SEAL TABBY POINT
AMERICAN CURL

SCOTTISH FOLD

FOLDED OR DROOPY EARS are commonly seen in dogs, but rarely occur in cats. However, in 1951 on a farm near Coupar Angus in Scotland, one kitten in a litter was born with pointed ears that gradually began to turn down towards its face. A local shepherd decided to establish these folded ears in a breed, giving rise to the Scottish Fold.

Small, tightly folded ears lie like little caps on the side of the head

LONGHAIRED FOLD
Although the original Scottish Folds had short coats, they must have carried a gene for long hair because subsequent litters contained long-coated kittens. Longhaired Folds have thick fur of medium length.

Short, stout legs can sometimes be abnormally thick

BLUE-CREAM
AND WHITE
SCOTTISH FOLD

FOLD FEATURES
The stocky body shape of Scottish Folds has been achieved by crossings with British Shorthairs. Scottish Folds are medium-sized and muscular, with large, round heads, emphasized by their folded ears.

Full, rounded cheeks and round eyes

Clear definition between blue and white areas of fur

Thick, powerful body is very compact

BLUE AND WHITE
SCOTTISH FOLD

Tail should measure at least two-thirds of the body length

CREAM CLASSIC
TABBY KITTENS

The kitten's ears are already beginning to fold.

SCOTTISH FOLD KITTENS
When first born, all Scottish Fold kittens have normal, pointed ears. After about two or three weeks the tips of the ears begin folding in towards the nose. Folded ears are a dominant mutation, meaning that if only one parent is a Fold, some of the kittens will also show this trait.

Scottish Folds can be bred in a wide variety of colours and patterns.

SCOTTISH FOLD FACTS

• Scottish Folds make placid and friendly pets. They are tolerant of other domestic animals, including dogs.

• The folded shape of these cats' ears does not make them more prone to ear infections than cats with normal ears.

• Scottish Folds are always bred to a cat from another breed to ensure that faults such as thick legs do not become a handicap.

ABYSSINIAN AND SOMALI

THE FIRST ABYSSINIAN CATS were brought to Britain in 1868 by soldiers returning from war in Abyssinia (now Ethiopia). Abyssinians look so similar to the cats in ancient Egyptian wallpaintings that they are believed to be related. The Somali breed originated from long-coated kittens in Abyssinian litters.

BLUE
ABYSSINIAN

Ticked fur is short, thick, and glossy

RUDDY
ABYSSINIAN

TRADITIONAL COLOURING
The original Abyssinian is known as the Usual, or Ruddy. It is sometimes called the "rabbit cat" because the orangish brown ticked colour of its coat is like a wild rabbit's. These athletic and lively cats have been popular pets for decades.

TWO-TONE COAT
The Blue Abyssinian used to be quite rare, but is now becoming more common. It has a steel blue-grey coat with an oatmeal-coloured undercoat. New colours are developed by cross-breeding with other types of cat.

CHOCOLATE
SILVER SOMALI

*Longer fur
on shoulders*

*Dark fur
extends up
back of legs*

TICKED FUR COLOUR

Both Abyssinians and Somalis have
what is described as ticked tabby fur.
Ticked fur colour is caused by light
and dark bands that alternate around
each hair. The tips
of the hairs are
always dark.
Depending on the
width and number
of the bands, the
coat can be
a darker or a
lighter shade.

TICKED FUR

LONGHAIRED SOMALI
These cats were named after
Somalia, which neighbours
Ethiopia, to reflect their
similarity to Abyssinians. They
differ in the length of fur, but
have the same body shape.

*Soft, dense fur
does not mat*

SOMALI CHARACTERISTICS
Abyssinians and Somalis can be born in
the same litter if the Abyssinian parents
carry a longhaired gene. However,
Somali parents produce only Somali
kittens. It can be 18 months before a
kitten's ticking is fully developed.

*The base coat is
white with blue
ticking.*

*Full,
bushy
tail*

BLUE SILVER SOMALI

MANX AND CYMRIC

LEGEND CLAIMS THAT 400 years ago, a Spanish galleon wrecked near the Isle of Man, off the coast of England, and tailless cats swam ashore. These were said to be ancestors of the Manx. But the mating of related cats on the island probably resulted in the tailless mutation.

NATIVE CAT
Manx cats are the symbol of the Isle of Man and feature on the island's coins. A cattery has been set up there to breed Manx.

TORTIE AND WHITE MANX

Shortened vertebrae make back look curved

TOTALLY TAILLESS
In the true Manx there is no tail at all, just a hollow at the end of the backbone. This type of Manx is known as a Rumpy.

ORANGE-EYED CYMRIC

Because the front legs are shorter than the back legs, the Manx has an odd, hopping walk.

LONGHAIRED MANX
The Cymric is a rare longhaired form of the Manx. Pronounced *kumric*, its unusual name is Welsh for "Wales". Like the Manx, it has a stocky, muscular body and is long-lived.

JAPANESE BOBTAIL

Cats with short tails have been known in Asia for 1,000 years. The Japanese Bobtail has a long history in Japan, although it is rare elsewhere. The Japanese believe that cats of this noisy and friendly breed bring good luck. Many Japanese homes are decorated with depictions of Bobtails. Their Japanese name means "beckoning cat" because they are known for raising a paw in greeting.

Pom-pom tail usually kept curled close to body

TORTOISESHELL AND WHITE JAPANESE BOBTAIL

Rabbit-like posture

TORTOISESHELL MANX

Shortened, stubby tail

Massive, muscular flanks

STUMPIES

Manx with short, moveable tails are called Stumpies. Longies are Manx with tails of almost the normal length. Tailless Rumpies must breed with Manx with some trace of tail or the kittens are at risk of spinal defects or even death.

PERSIAN LONGHAIR AND EXOTIC

LONG-COATED CATS were known in Persia (now Iran)
centuries before they were introduced to Europe. This
explains how the large, fluffy,
flat-faced breed got its name.
Exotics have a shorter history.
They were developed in the
1960s as shorthaired
versions of
Persians.

POPULAR VICTORIAN PET
Persians took part in the first modern
cat show in 1871 in Britain. Queen
Victoria kept Blue Persians, which
helped to make this breed very popular
during the 19th century both in Britain
and in the United States.

*Shape of the body
is all but hidden by
the thick coat*

Short, bushy tail

PERSIAN FEATURES
Breeders have emphasized certain qualities in
Persians. The body is massive and stocky, the head
is round, and the face extremely compressed.
Persians have the longest and
densest fur of any
cat breed.

*In bi-colour Persians,
white markings cover
one-third to one-half
of the coat.*

CREAM AND
WHITE BI-COLOUR
PERSIAN

Short, plush coat is easy to care for

EXOTIC SHORTHAIR
Except for its short, dense coat, the Exotic resembles the Persian in almost every respect. These cats are lively and friendly and come in many colours.

Thick tail with blunt tip

Strong, stubby legs

Small round ears with tufts of fur inside

SHADED
GOLDEN EXOTIC

CHOCOLATE
PERSIAN

LILAC
PERSIAN

Broad, muscular chest

COLOUR RANGE
Persians come in over 30 colours. Their coats can be one pure colour, bi-coloured, mixed colours, or patterned. Persians with Himalayan markings are called Colourpoints.

NEWLY CREATED COLOURS
The Persian's lush coat has been made increasingly glamorous by breeders in search of ever more distinctive colours. The warm, pinkish grey coat of this Lilac is a dilute, or lighter, form of chocolate.

Tufted paws

SIAMESE AND BALINESE

THE SVELTE AND REGAL SIAMESE is one of the best-known cats in the world. This type of cat has been recorded in Thailand (formerly Siam) since the 14th century. The Siamese's longhaired relative, the Balinese, is named after the graceful, swaying dancers of Bali.

ANCIENT HISTORY
For centuries, cats with Siamese markings have been painted in Thailand. Legend claims that the first Siamese had crossed eyes from staring at a vase they were given to guard.

Head is triangular, with large ears and almond-shaped eyes

SEAL TORTIE POINT SIAMESE

Long, slender body with fine bone structure

Tortoiseshell patterning disrupts the point markings

POINT PATTERN
Siamese have pale bodies with darker-coloured points on the face, legs, feet, and tail. All Siamese kittens are light-coloured at birth and develop points over time.

• In hot climates, Siamese have points of a lighter shade.

• Siamese are prone to polydactylism (having extra toes). One Siamese cat was born with 26 toes instead of the usual 18!

BALINESE

This recent breed is the result of pairings between Siamese and Angoras. Balinese have the same elegant body shape as Siamese cats, but with longer fur and a distinctive plumed tail. They are less vocal than their relatives.

Points occur on parts of the body with cooler temperatures

Long, wedge-shaped face

BLUE TABBY POINT BALINESE

Silky fur grows up to 5 cm (2 in) long

CLOSE RELATION

A popular and friendly breed, the Burmese came about from a mating between a Siamese cat and a brown cat from Burma. Brown cats had been living in Burmese Buddhist temples since the 15th century. Burmese are now bred in many colours.

Slightly stockier body than the Siamese

CHOCOLATE BURMESE

LONGHAIRED CATS

ABOUT LONGHAIRED CATS

APART FROM RARE EXCEPTIONS, wild cats do not have long fur. It would be a disadvantage, getting tangled and caught in undergrowth. However, a few types of domestic cats evolved thick coats. Breeders who desired this trait have since created many longhaired varieties by crossing shorthairs with long-coated cats.

NATURALLY EVOLVED COAT
The Norwegian Forest Cat is an example of a breed that developed long fur for its chilly habitat. A layer of warm down lies underneath the waterproof outer coat.

Pressing on the thick fur leaves an indentation mark.

PRIZE-WINNING LONGHAIR
Cats with long coats were first brought to the West in the 1600s. By the early 1900s, longhaired cats like this one were winning cat shows.

BLUE TORTIE TABBY
AND WHITE
NORWEGIAN
FOREST CAT

PRETTY OR PRACTICAL?

Long hair is not just an attractive feature that has been created artificially. Dense, long fur is water-repellent, protecting the cat from wet and cold weather. Persians, like the one shown here, have been bred to possess the longest coats of any cats. Their fur can be 10 cm (4 in) long.

SEMI-LONGHAIR

The Birman's coat is typical of the fur type known as semi-longhair. These cats have a long, silky top coat and a very fine undercoat. The Angora is another example of a semi-longhaired breed.

Sparse undercoat makes the Birman's fur unlikely to mat

LILAC POINT BIRMAN

GROOMING A LONGHAIRED CAT

All cats like to keep tidy, but longhairs need extra help. Daily grooming is essential if you own one. Otherwise, not only will the fur become matted and soiled, but you will be faced with loose hairs all around the home. You may also need to wash the cat.

Use a bristle brush.

Some cats enjoy being groomed.

Regular grooming prevents knots.

TURKISH ANGORA

ONE OF THE OLDEST longhaired breeds, the Turkish Angora is from Ankara, in Turkey. In the 16th century, Turkish sultans sent these cats as gifts to European nobles. Recently, the breed was saved from extinction by the efforts of the Ankara Zoo.

BLACK TORTIE
SMOKE
TURKISH ANGORA

Soft, light, silky coat

FATHER OF THE TURKS
This portrait shows the Turkish leader Kemal Atatürk in 1921. Legend held that when he died he would be reincarnated as a deaf white cat, probably referring to an Angora.

NOBLE APPEARANCE
Turkish Angoras have lithe, graceful bodies and long, plume-like tails. Compared to the size of the body, the head is small and angular. These cats have friendly and playful temperaments.

Full, tapering tail

TRADITIONAL TYPE

The first Turkish Angoras were white. These pure white cats have been bred in Turkey for over 500 years and are still known by their Turkish name, *Ankara kedi*. Traditionally, cats of this ancient breed have eyes of two different colours, one orange and the other blue. Deafness on the side of the blue eye is likely because of a genetic weakness common in blue-eyed white cats.

ODD-EYED WHITE TURKISH ANGORA

Almond-shaped eyes

Pure white coat

Round, short head with widely spaced ears

Long, angular head

Slender, tubular body

CINNAMON ANGORA

ARTIFICIALLY CREATED ANGORAS

In the 1960s, breeders created a new kind of Angora. This breed differs from the Turkish type in that they look like their Oriental ancestors, are more vocal, and have larger litters.

Angoras look more sleek in the summer when they shed their winter coat.

WHITE ANGORA

TURKISH VAN

THE "SWIMMING CAT", or Turkish Van, has been domesticated in Turkey for several centuries, but was unknown elsewhere until 1955. Unlike other long-coated cats, the Turkish Van has no undercoat, so it dries quickly after a swim.

LAKE VAN
Turkish Vans originated in the region of Lake Van in Turkey. The area is stiflingly hot in summer and freezing cold in winter. These cats have adapted to shed most of their winter coat in hot weather.

AUBURN TURKISH VANS

Eyes can be amber, blue, or odd-eyed, with pink rims

TURKISH VAN PATTERN
These cats have a distinctive chalky-white colour with coloured areas on the head and tail. The white patch on the centre of the head is said by Turkish people to symbolize the thumbprint of Allah, the god of Islam.

Turkish Vans are affectionate and lively.

Short, wedge-shaped head with large ears

CREAM
TURKISH VAN

SWIMMING CAT
Although most cats hate getting wet, Turkish Vans will swim readily. Their legs propel them forwards, while their tail acts like a boat's rudder. Why this behaviour evolved is a mystery, but long ago the cats may have been attracted to the fish darting in the shallows of Lake Van.

Feathery, brush-like tail

COVETED CAT
Auburn and cream are the two most common varieties of the Turkish Van. These cats have sturdy bodies and are good climbers. They also have unusual, melodious voices. Since these cats were first brought to the West by two photographers, this breed has become popular in many countries.

Darker rings may encircle tail, particularly in kittens

BIRMAN

FROM ITS FABLED PAST in Southeast Asia to its long journey to Europe in the 1900s, the Birman has a colourful history. This ancient breed is known as the sacred cat of Burma because of the mystical legends that surround the origins of its unique white paw markings.

BLUE POINT
BIRMAN

The kittens' points will darken as they age.

DISTINCTIVE PATTERNS
Symmetrical white "gloves" cover the Birman's front paws. White fur also extends up their back legs, like gauntlets.

Pure white "gloves"

BIRMAN BEGINNINGS
In 1919, two travellers brought the first Birmans to Europe. Buddhist priests had given the cats to the couple as thanks for their help in defending a temple. Only the female cat survived the tiring trip to the West. She produced a litter of kittens soon afterwards in France.

BLUE POINT
KITTENS

The Blue Point is one of the traditional colours of this breed.

Medium-length fur is longer on back

SACRED CAT OF BURMA

The Birman is said to have gained its markings during a battle at a Buddhist temple, like the one above. The story claims that one of the white temple cats touched a dying priest. Its paws remained snow white, its head, tail, and legs became brown, and its back turned golden.

Long body has a strong, stocky build

ORIGINAL BIRMAN

The Seal Point is the original type of Birman. The fur on its back has a golden glow. Legend claims that during its miraculous transformation the temple cat's eyes changed from yellow to sapphire blue.

SEAL POINT
BIRMAN

MAINE COON

THESE CATS were the first long-coated breed to originate in North America. In the 1700s, the Maine Coon's shorthaired ancestors sailed from Europe. These were ships' cats, brought aboard to kill rats. The Maine Coon's odd habit of sleeping in tiny, cramped spaces might relate to its seafaring heritage.

WEATHERPROOFED COAT
The warm, dense coat of the Maine Coon developed to give these cats good protection during the bitter winters of Maine.

Large, solid body

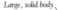

Maine Coons make an unusual chirping sound.

Sometimes these cats use their front paws to pick up food.

SILVER TABBY
MAINE COON

70

SILVER TABBY

Winter ruff

RACCOON
This North
American mammal
is often known as
the "coon". Its
markings, long coat,
and striped tail have given rise
to a myth that Maine Coons
descended from raccoons.

WINTER AND SUMMER COATS
The Maine Coon's shaggy coat is
noticeably longer in the winter,
when it has a distinct ruff of fur
around the neck (above). Its thick
coat protects the cat in cold wind
and weather. In the summer, the cat
sheds much of this fur (below).

*Cat grooms long,
bushy tail by
wrapping it round
front leg and
swivelling to lick it*

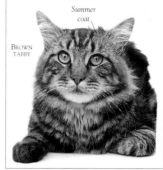

Summer
coat

BROWN
TABBY

BIGGEST BREED
Maine Coons are some of the
largest domestic cats. They are
very muscular, with powerful
legs and broad chests. This
makes them well suited to
outdoor life. Males are bigger
than females; they may weigh
up to 8 kg (18 lb).

NORWEGIAN AND SIBERIAN FOREST CATS

BOTH THESE WILD-LOOKING BREEDS come from northern Europe, where the winters are icy cold. This would explain how their warm, two-layer coats might have naturally evolved. Another theory suggests that Norwegian Forest Cats may be distantly related to Persians or Angoras brought to the area in the 1500s.

BLUE TORTIE
SMOKE NORWEGIAN
FOREST CAT

RUGGED COAT
Having a double-layered coat helps these cats stay dry, because water runs off the outer layer of their fur. After a thorough soaking, Forest Cats are dry in 15 minutes. If they live indoors or in hot climates, their fur becomes softer and shorter.

SKILFUL HUNTER
These intelligent cats are adventurous hunters. They wander widely in an area, so they need a lot of room. Forest Cats are superb, agile climbers of rocks and trees.

BLACK SMOKE AND
WHITE NORWEGIAN
FOREST CAT

SMOKE FUR COLOUR

This coloration results from a pale undercoat combined with dark outer guard hairs. As the cat moves, its undercoat becomes visible through the longer guard hairs. The contrast is most obvious in cats of darker colours, particularly black. A unique shimmery effect is created.

SMOKE FUR

NORSE CATS

Cats were important in Viking life. Norse mythology tells of enchanted cats that roamed the Scandinavian forests. The Norse love goddess Freya is shown here on a chariot pulled by giant cats.

Long fur on sides of face

SIBERIAN FOREST CAT

These cats are rare outside Russia, where they have been bred for over 1,000 years. Some believe that Siberian Forest Cats were the original longhairs, and all other long-coated breeds are their descendants.

Profuse tail and furry hindquarters

Tabby markings may be the result of matings with wild cats.

SIBERIAN FOREST CAT

RAGDOLL

THESE CATS' STRANGE characteristic of relaxing totally when they are touched fuelled the already widespread rumour that Ragdolls feel no pain. This myth first originated when the queen that founded the breed gave birth after being injured in a road accident. However, there is no doubt that Ragdolls are as sensitive to pain as any cat.

BLUE MITTED
RAGDOLL

"Boots" of white
fur on paws

RAGDOLL
KITTEN

ORIGINS OF THE BREED
Ragdolls were developed in the 1960s by a U.S. breeder who wanted to create the perfect house pet. The cats are unusual in that they were bred largely to cultivate their loving temperaments. The Ragdoll was the first breed in history to receive its own trademark.

It takes three years for a young Ragdoll to take on its adult size and colour.

YOUNG RAGDOLL
The offspring of Ragdolls are born almost pure white. Their points start to develop after about a week. The shade of the coat varies throughout the cat's life, depending on the time of year. The fur often becomes paler in summer.

Inverted white "V" on face

SEAL
BI-COLOUR
RAGDOLL

Odd white spots on coloured areas

LUXURIOUS COAT
The silky fur of this breed is medium-length and quite dense. The coat is much longer in the winter, particularly around the neck, where the longer fur looks like a bib. The coat is visibly shorter in summer.

Broad, muscular body

Loose pad of fat on underside

SEAL POINT
RAGDOLL

Large, blue eyes

TOLERANT PET
The relaxed nature of these cats gave them their name – they go as limp as a rag doll when they are held. All three varieties of this breed have docile personalities and become totally devoted to their owners.

These cats love children.

IMPOSING SIZE
Ragdolls are one of the largest domestic cat breeds. Mature males can span up to 90 cm (3 ft) when their front and back legs are outstretched. They can reach an average weight of 9 kg (20 lb), while females tend to be lighter – about 6.5 kg (15 lb).

Relaxes completely in owner's arms

NON-PEDIGREE

CATS WITH LONG COATS are not always glamorous, pure-bred show cats. In fact, the humble non-pedigree cat is far more common. There is an infinite variety of longhaired non-pedigree cats. They come in every shape, size, colour, and pattern. Each individual cat is totally unique since it has not been specially bred to conform to a set standard.

TABBY MARKINGS

It is more common for non-pedigree cats to have tabby patterns than any other type of markings. This is because tabby is the natural pattern of a cat's coat. In non-pedigree cats, tabby markings are random and individual for every different cat.

Non-pedigree longhairs usually have shorter fur than pure-breds.

RED TABBY, OR "GINGER"

STRIKING APPEARANCE

Some non-pedigree cats are distinctive enough to look like show cats. Black-tipped fur gives this cat its silvery shade. Such cats may be used to found new types of pedigree breeds.

TIPPED FUR COLOUR

In this type of coat just the tips of the long guard hairs are coloured, while the rest of the hair is white. Tipping may occur in the shorter awn hairs as well. The result is a trace of colour on the fur, which creates a sparkling effect as the cat moves. Tipping is not commonly seen in non-pedigree cats.

TIPPED FUR

SILVER AND WHITE

POPULAR PET

Non-pedigree cats are far more popular among pet owners than their pure-bred relatives. They have friendly dispositions and are generally hardy, rarely suffering the health problems that some pedigree cats can be prone to.

WITCH'S FAMILIAR

In medieval times, cats were thought to be linked with witches. This led to thousands of cats being persecuted all over Europe during this period.

Non-pedigree cats can be obtained from humane societies.

Tortoiseshell cats make excellent mothers.

TORTIE AND WHITE

SHORTHAIRED CATS

ABOUT SHORTHAIRED CATS

LIKE THEIR WILD RELATIVES, most domestic cats have short fur. Cats with short coats are popular because they require little grooming, so are easy to look after. Short fur is also genetically dominant; if a long-coated cat mates with a pure shorthair, the kittens will have short coats.

PETS OF THE PAST
Non-pedigree cats, or "moggies", with short hair have been popular for centuries. Even today, in spite of the growing number of pure-bred cats, moggies are still the preferred pets.

RED POINT
TONKINESE

Blue-green eyes

SPOTTED MIST
New breeds are constantly being created, whether the crossings are planned or occur by chance. The Spotted Mist is the first breed from Australia. It was developed from crossings based mainly on Burmese and Abyssinians. Their coats are sleek, fine, and delicately spotted.

Short, close-lying fur keeps cat cool in hot climates

VARIETIES OF SHORTHAIRED COATS

Shorthaired coats can be sleek and fine, like the Siamese, or thick and plush like the British Shorthair. Breeds like the Rex have short, curly fur, while the Manx has a dense, double-layered coat that stands out from its body.

ANCESTOR OF ALL BREEDS

The African wild cat is believed to be the original species from which all of today's domestic breeds evolved. Thousands of years ago, African wild cats were probably attracted to ancient Egyptian settlements, where they fed on mice and rats in grain stores. Eventually some became quite tame.

Crossing a Burmese with a Chinchilla Longhair created a soft, dense coat.

BROWN TIPPED BURMILLA

Coat is soft, with a natural, glossy sheen

Body shape is a cross between a Siamese and a Burmese

FOREIGN SHORTHAIR

Pedigree shorthairs fall into three main categories: British, American, or Foreign Shorthairs. The Tonkinese is a Foreign Shorthair. Its soft fur has the same texture as a mink's, so they are often known as Minks in the U.S.A.

BRITISH SHORTHAIR

THIS STURDY CAT is a popular choice among pedigree pet owners. Intelligent, friendly, and placid, British Shorthairs make good companions. The breed was developed in the late 1800s from the best of the non-pedigree cats roaming the streets of 19th-century Britain.

CREAM AND WHITE BRITISH SHORTHAIR

Short, strong legs

"M"-shaped marking on forehead is usual in tabbies

This is now the rarest bi-colour combination.

STOCKY CAT

A massive, compact body and a broad, round head are characteristic of the British Shorthair's body shape. This shape is described as cobby. British Shorthairs are larger than most non-pedigree varieties. The males in particular are tough-looking and muscular, but they are home-loving cats with attractive natures and soft, plush coats.

SILVER SPOTTED BRITISH SHORTHAIR

Fur should be crisp and dense

CHOCOLATE KITTEN

LILAC KITTEN

COLOUR POINTED BRITISH SHORTHAIR
In the 1980s, crossing Colourpoint
Longhairs with British Shorthairs
gave rise to a cobby breed with
points. Friendly and even-tempered,
Colour Pointed British Shorthairs
are calmer than pure-bred Siamese.
Their placid natures should ensure
that they steadily gain in popularity.

BLUE POINT BRITISH
SHORTHAIR

Blue
eyes

Coat is short, with
good contrast between points
and body colour

ARRAY OF COLOURS
British Shorthairs come in a vast
range of colours and patterns. Self
(solid) colour cats, especially the
British Blue, are the most popular.
New colours, like lilac and chocolate,
have recently been created by
crossings with Persian Longhairs.

TABBY ORIGINS
Tamed cats with spotted markings date
back to ancient Egyptian times. The
word "tabby" derives from the old
al Attabiya quarter of Baghdad,
Iraq, where a black and white
patterned silk (known in
the West as "tabbi")
was once made.

Barred tabby
pattern is broken
into spots

Barring
on legs

Thick tail
with black
tip

SNOWSHOE

WHITE MARKINGS superimposed on a Siamese pattern are the Snowshoe's trademark. This relatively new American breed was not widely known until the 1980s. These cats have active, sunny dispositions, and are gaining popularity in many countries.

SNOWSHOE KITTEN

Bright blue eyes

DISTINCTIVE MARKINGS
Snowshoe kittens are born pure white. Over two years, they develop darker points on the head, legs, and tail, along with the white markings characteristic of the breed. The kitten above already shows the distinctive white paws which earned Snowshoes the nickname "Silver Laces".

Dark points contrast with white markings

ORIGINS OF THE SNOWSHOE
This breed was founded from three Siamese kittens born with white feet. Some breeders were worried that if these kittens' white markings became established they might spread into Siamese bloodlines. The breed was developed in spite of these concerns, using American Shorthairs to give the Snowshoe a large, strong, muscular build.

SEAL AND WHITE POINT SNOWSHOE

Front paws are white to ankle

SHOWING CATS

Snowshoes, like the one pictured here, are now breaking into show circles. Cat shows are the main way in which standards for breeds are determined. Cats are judged on markings, coat condition, body shape, and health.

YOUNG SNOWSHOE

SIZE DIFFERENCE

There is usually a big difference in size between male and female Snowshoes. Toms tend to be much larger, weighing up to 5.4 kg (12 lb). Males develop prominent jowls as they mature.

Strong, muscular body

Colour is darker in older cats and in cold climates

This young Snowshoe shows its Siamese heritage.

White markings on back legs extend above the knee

Long tail

AMERICAN SHORTHAIR

DESCENDED FROM THE FIRST CATS brought to North America by European settlers in the 1500s, the American Shorthair remains a tough, hardy cat. It is independent and strongly built, a legacy from the frontier cats that lived in the early American settlements. These skilled mousers were not specially bred in their first years, so they evolved along natural lines. Only since the early 1900s have these cats been standardized into a breed.

SHADED SILVER
AMERICAN
SHORTHAIR

Dark shading on back

TYPICAL AMERICAN
Compared to its British counterpart, the American Shorthair is larger and more powerful. It has a less rounded face, a longer nose, and longer legs than a British Shorthair. The fur is very short and coarse, adapted for a harsh outdoor life. This breed normally has a robust and healthy constitution.

Thick fur with hard texture

Longer tail than its British cousin

COLONIAL CATS

For centuries, ships carried cats to kill rats. The cats would disembark at ports around the world, or were brought ashore by settlers anxious to protect grain stores in their new homes.

SHADED FUR COLOUR

A coat that is shaded has dark outer guard hairs and a white undercoat. On the guard hairs, the dark shade extends partway down each hair from its tip, but never reaches the root. Shaded coats are darker than tipped, but lighter than smoke fur. The white undercoat is revealed when the cat moves.

SHADED FUR

Bright blue eyes

EXPERT HUNTER

Because it developed largely without human interference, the American Shorthair is well adapted for survival. Its short, square jaws are strong, ideal for catching prey. Having to fend for themselves has given these cats streetwise intelligence.

RED AND WHITE
VAN TABBY
AMERICAN
SHORTHAIR

Long, muscular legs help the cat make high leaps.

AMERICAN WIREHAIR

FRIZZY FUR that looks as if it is standing on end gives the American Wirehair its unique appearance. These uncommon cats originated from a male wiry haired kitten born in 1967 in New York state, U.S.A. This unusual breed is mostly unknown outside North America.

LONDON BOMB SITE
In Britain during World War II, derelict buildings were colonized by feral cats. Wiry-coated cats were first recorded at sites like these. However, they were not bred and soon died out.

Tabby pattern looks raised because of wiry fur

SILVER MACKEREL TABBY AMERICAN WIREHAIR

CRIMPED COAT
The American Wirehair's guard hairs are thin and bent at the ends. Every hair is crimped, making the coat springy and dense. The fur feels like lamb's-wool to the touch. Wirehair kittens are born with tight, curly coats. It takes four or five months before their fur takes on its adult crimped texture.

Dense fur can be wavy or may even form ringlets

Round head with prominent cheekbones

Fur under chin and underneath body is less coarse than rest of coat

Striped pattern is known as "mackerel" because it looks like a fish skeleton

ROBUST BREED
American Shorthairs were used to develop Wirehairs, so they share a similar body shape. Wirehairs, like this brown and white tabby, are slightly smaller. These cats are long-lived and have playful and curious natures.

Hair in ears is also crimped

BROWN AND WHITE CLASSIC TABBY

CURLY WHISKERS
Even a Wirehair's whiskers are crimped and curly. If its fur gets wet, it takes several days for it to regain its springiness. The coat requires very little extra attention.

EUROPEAN SHORTHAIR

CATS HAVE LIVED in Europe for thousands of years, but the European Shorthair only became a distinct breed in 1982. Before then, it was considered identical to the British Shorthair. There are only slight differences between these cats and their close British cousins.

TORTIE SMOKE
EUROPEAN
SHORTHAIR

ORDINARY ORIGINS

This breed developed from non-pedigree European cats. Later, these cats were crossed with British Shorthairs to increase body size. Now that they are a separate breed, these crossings are no longer allowed, and European Shorthairs are evolving along different lines.

EUROPEAN
SHORTHAIR FACTS

• These athletic and stocky cats make good pets, but they retain a strong instinct to hunt.

• There is a rare pure white form of European Shorthair with blue eyes that, unlike most other blue-eyed white cats, is not deaf.

If these cats spend a lot of time in strong sunlight, the black in their fur may turn a rusty brown.

Compact, rounded paws

ANCIENT FRENCH SHORTHAIR
Here at the monastery of La Grande Chartreuse, near Grenoble in France, medieval monks bred the ancient and rare Chartreux breed for its fur. These blue-grey cats are easily mistaken for Blue European Shorthairs because they look so similar. Chartreux cats almost became extinct in the 1920s.

CREAM SHADED CAMEO TABBY EUROPEAN SHORTHAIR

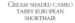

Tabby markings become less distinct during moulting

DISTINCTIVE FEATURES
Today's European Shorthairs have slightly longer heads and sleeker body shapes than British Shorthairs. These cats are bred in many colours and patterns. They are hardy and good-natured, but are currently not as well known as their British and American counterparts.

Thick, short tail

REX BREEDS

UNLIKE ANY OTHER BREED, Rexes have distinctive curly coats. The fur is short and wavy, like the Rex rabbit after which these breeds were named. Crimped coats are a rare but natural mutation, so this kind of fur crops up from time to time in cats in various countries. Today, however, just these three Rex breeds with curly coats are widely kept as pets.

Large ears have rounded tips and are covered with fine fur

CREAM DEVON REX

The whiskers are crinkly and can be fragile.

Oval-shaped, widely spaced eyes

THE FIRST DEVON REX
Kirlee, the original smoky-grey Devon Rex, appeared in 1960 after a mating between a pet cat and a large, curly-coated cat in the neighbourhood. *Kirlee* was born in Devon, a western county of England. Devon Rexes differ from Cornish Rexes in that their fur is more twisted.

PIXIE FACE
The Devon Rex's head is unique. These cats have short, broad faces, large eyes, and prominent cheeks. These features, combined with their large, bat-like ears, give them a mischievous appearance, which is in keeping with their playful characters.

Both sexes have jowls.

MOST RECENT REX

The Selkirk is the latest breed of Rex, appearing in 1987. The unique texture of the coat is fully developed 10 months after birth. Selkirk kittens shed their first curly coat and have sparse, wiry fur for two to three months before they develop their adult coats.

Thick, plush coat with loose curls all over body

BLUE CREAM
SELKIRK REX

Siamese-type markings

CORNISH REX

This breed's coat is exceptionally soft and short since it lacks guard hairs. However, this gives the cat little protection in cold and wet weather. Curly fur and a habit of wagging its tail when contented gives the cat its nickname, "poodle cat".

Rippled fur can be groomed by stroking with the hand

The coat flattens when wet, only gradually becoming curly as it dries out.

CHOCOLATE
POINT SI-REX
CORNISH REX

Body is thin, but these cats have a tendency to get fat

SPHYNX

ARGUABLY THE MOST BIZARRE of any cat breed,
controversy surrounds the Sphynx. Some people
believe that the hairless Sphynx
should no longer be bred, as its
lack of fur may be bad for the
cat's health. Hairlessness can occur
naturally in animals like dogs and
mice, but it is a very rare trait.

BLACK AND
WHITE SPHYNX

*Skin has a
suede-like
texture*

SPHYNX FACTS

• Lack of fur leaves
these cats vulnerable to
cold and sunburn.

• The Sphynx often
rests with one paw held
off the ground.

• The Sphynx is warm
to the touch, hence its
nickname, "suede hot
water bottle".

BALD BODY
Modern Sphynxes
originated from a mutant
kitten born to a black and
white cat in Canada in 1966.
The colour of a Sphynx comes
from pigmentation in its skin.
The pink areas correspond to
what would be white fur in a
cat with a coat, and the dark
skin with what would be dark fur.

BROWN AND
WHITE SPHYNX

WORRIED BROW
The Sphynx has an angular face, with
wrinkled skin on the forehead. The ears are
very large and triangular, with rounded tips.
The whiskers are either short and stunted
or they may be completely absent.

*Eye
colour
should
complement
skin colour*

*Pronounced
cheek bones*

BROWN AND
WHITE SPHYNX
KITTEN

BORN FURRY
A young Sphynx is born with
a light covering of fur. This is
gradually lost as it grows older,
leaving the body entirely hairless
except for the tail, face, ears, and
feet. The kitten's loose and
wrinkly skin will become
smoother with age.

*Barrel-shaped
chest*

*Each cat has a
unique pattern.*

*Tuft of hair on
tip of tail*

*Sphynxes are unusual
in that they sweat, so
they need to be cleaned
with a damp sponge.*

AZTEC CAT
HEAD
SCULPTURE

AZTEC ORIGINS
Hairless cats were first bred by the
Aztecs, who lived in Mexico in the
14–15th centuries. This sculpture is
evidence that the Aztecs domesticated
cats. They also developed a hairless dog
breed that still exists, but the early
hairless cats are extinct.

CALIFORNIA SPANGLED

UNIQUELY LAUNCHED in the 1986 Christmas catalogue of Neiman-Marcus, a well-known American store, this breed created a stir from the start. In keeping with its wild appearance, the California Spangled is intelligent and active. Interest in these cats is so great that there is a long waiting list for Spangled kittens.

ENVIRONMENTAL SYMBOL
The idea behind the breeding of the California Spangled was to raise concern among cat-lovers about the plight of the world's wild cats. Hence, these cats' lean, muscular bodies and striking spotted coats are reminiscent of wild cats.

Spots can be round, square, or triangular

GOLD CALIFORNIA
SPANGLED

Paul Casey holding Yuma, an 8-month-old Silver

INSPIRATION FOR THE BREED
A leopard he saw on a visit to Africa inspired Paul Casey to create the California Spangled. He hoped to spur people into acting to protect endangered wild cats, but only domestic cats were used to develop this breed. It took six generations to achieve the features he desired.

PURPOSEFUL BREEDER
In 1971, Paul Casey, a scriptwriter from California, began his quest to develop a wild-looking breed. He named the first cats after Native American tribes.

Rounded ears set back on head, away from face

SPANGLED COAT
The patterned coat of this breed is paramount. Each variety has nearly identical markings, differing only in colour. The one exception is the "Snow Leopard", which is born pure white and develops spots gradually.

BLUE CALIFORNIA SPANGLED

EGYPTIAN MAU

THIS RARE BREED claims a lineage stretching back thousands of years to ancient Egypt. The markings of the Egyptian Mau are similar to those of cats depicted on Egyptian scrolls and tomb paintings. The modern Egyptian Mau originated in the 1950s from a spotted cat brought to Italy from Cairo, Egypt by a princess.

ANCIENT EGYPTIAN CAT SCULPTURE (600 B.C.)

SILVER EGYPTIAN MAU KITTEN

Mau kittens have less distinct markings than adults.

SACRED CAT
The ancient Egyptians believed cats were divine. They worshipped the cat goddess, Bastet, among other deities, and made sculptures and other artefacts in her honour. Killing a cat was punishable by death.

Rounded face and large, pointed ears

BLACK SMOKE KITTEN

NOBLE BACKGROUND
"Mau" was the ancient Egyptian word for the sacred domestic cat. Today's breed was developed mainly in the U.S.A. These cats come in three colours – silver, bronze, and black smoke, which is the darkest variety.

SILVER
EGYPTIAN
MAU

ATTRACTIVE EYES
One of the most appealing features of Egyptian Maus are their unusual green eyes. This colour takes up to two years to develop fully, and may turn a paler green as the cats age. The eyes are oval and very large. Their slanted shape is emphasized by dark lines running across the cat's cheeks.

Characteristic "M"-shaped tabby marking in centre of head

"Mascara lines" on face are reminiscent of ancient Egyptian face make-up

ORIENTAL SPOTTED TABBY
Confusingly, this cat was once called an Egyptian Mau even though it is a separate breed. Now classed as an Oriental Shorthair, this type of tabby developed from Siamese cats and has no connection with Egypt.

Spots are round and evenly distributed on the body

Dark stripe runs down the back, breaking into bands on the tail

OCICAT

ONE OF THE NEWER shorthaired breeds, the wild-looking Ocicat emerged in the U.S.A. in 1964. The breed came about from an unplanned mating between a Siamese and an Abyssinian–Siamese cross. The name "Ocicat" was derived from a combination of the breed's two previous names: "Accicat", reflecting its accidental origins, and "Ocelette" because of its resemblance to an ocelot.

CHOCOLATE
OCICAT

Almond-shaped eyes

Large, strong body

Muscular legs with dark markings

Powerful, oval-shaped paws

CUB-LIKE KITTENS
Young Ocicats are born with delightful spotted patterning, although their markings are less distinct than those of adult Ocicats. The kittens' coats begin to change about five weeks after birth. The first Ocicat kitten's resemblance to a wild cub so enchanted the original owner that she went on to found the breed.

Glossy, fine, short fur is ticked with at least two bands of colour

SILVER
OCICAT

Black line encircles brick-red nose

Long, patterned tail ends in a black tip

DISTINCTIVE COAT
Dark lines extend around the neck and legs. The rest of the body is covered in spots about the size of thumbprints. Each cat's pattern is individual.

Dark markings are clear on lighter background

WILD OCELOT
The Ocicat's markings are said to look like those of this small wild cat, which ranges from the southern U.S.A. southwards as far as Argentina. In some areas, they have been heavily hunted for their beautiful fur.

Unlike other cats, ocelots may live in pairs.

OCELOT

The markings are highly individual.

OCICAT FEATURES
The body shape of the Ocicat is partway between the svelte Oriental and the sturdy American Shorthair. The breed's large, well-muscled body gives an impression of power and strength.

Ocicats are friendly and have a reputation for dog-like loyalty to their owners.

ORIENTAL SHORTHAIR

LITHE AND ELEGANT, this breed is a successful attempt at creating Siamese cats without pointed markings. Oriental Shorthairs are intelligent and lively and come in a huge range of colours and patterns. These stylish cats are steadily growing in popularity.

Oyster-like marking on flank is a feature of all classic tabbies

CHOCOLATE CLASSIC TABBY ORIENTAL SHORTHAIR

Long, svelte body with sleek fur

Bracelets of chocolate-brown fur on legs

Delicate, oval paws

Long, slender legs

SVELTE SHAPE

Like the Siamese, this breed has a thin, almost tubular, body shape. Slender legs and a long, narrow tail add to their sleek elegance. Orientals are exceedingly agile; they can jump, run, and climb with graceful ease.

HUGE VARIETY

In recent years, the number of different types of Oriental Shorthair has expanded greatly. Using the myriad colours and patterns available, it is estimated that 400 varieties could ultimately be created.

ORIENTAL SHORTHAIR FACTS

• Almost every variety of Oriental Shorthair has green eyes.

• These cats are quieter than their Siamese ancestors, but are just as demanding.

• In 1951, the first Oriental Shorthair (a Havana) was created.

FOREIGN BLACK, OR EBONY

The Ebony is one of the original Oriental varieties. It arose from crosses between Siamese cats and Russian Blues, and has silky, jet-black fur. Like other Orientals, it is active and energetic and can be trained to walk on a lead.

Angular head with large, pointed ears

CHOCOLATE TORTIE ORIENTAL SHORTHAIR

FOREIGN RED

Solid (or "self") coloured types of this breed are described in Britain as Foreign Shorthairs. Strictly, the term Oriental Shorthair is used only for varieties that have patterns, such as tortoiseshells or tabbies.

Random, mottled pattern

Close-lying fur is short, fine, and glossy

KORAT

PRIZED IN ITS NATIVE SIAM (now called Thailand) for centuries, the Korat is one of the most ancient of all cat breeds. These dusky blue-silver cats have a regal and well-recorded history in Southeast Asia. The Thai people call the Korat "Si-sawat" because of its reputation for bringing its owners good fortune and happiness.

KING RAMA V
It is said that Rama V, king of Siam from 1873 to 1910 named the Korat after the Thai province where these attractive cats have been kept for centuries.

KORAT

Fine, silky fur lies close to the body

LUSTROUS COAT
A Korat's fur is a lush blue tipped with silver. This gives the coat a silvery sheen. These cats lack a warm undercoat because of their tropical origins, and must be protected from getting chilled.

ANCIENT HISTORY
Korats are lovingly and poetically described in the Southeast Asian *Cat Book Poems*, written between 1350 and 1767. One ancient Thai legend claims that the breed was originally developed by two hermits.

Medium-sized, lithe, and muscular body

104

LUCKY WEDDING GIFTS

Because Korats are considered symbols of good luck in Thailand, they are popular gifts for newlywed couples. It is claimed that in the past Korats were used in rain-making ceremonies. These sweet-natured, home-loving cats have also gained many followers since their introduction to the West in the late 1950s.

Traditional Thai bride and groom

THAI WEDDING CEREMONY

Round, luminous green eyes and distinctive heart-shaped face

KORATS

Korats have affectionate and playful temperaments.

RUSSIAN SHORTHAIR

THIS NOBLE BREED has a singularly soft, plush coat.
The Russian Shorthair evolved near the Arctic
Circle, farther north than any other
breed. Mystery surrounds its origins,
though there is much evidence that
it is a native Russian cat. Originally,
all Russian Shorthairs were
blue, but today new
colours are being
developed.

RUSSIAN
BLUE

FAMOUS RUSSIAN
The most famous Russian Blue
was the pampered pet of Tsar
Nicholas I, emperor of Russia
(1825-55). Although these cats
are considered portents of good
luck in Russia, the breed has
become rare in its native land.

*Evenly blue-coloured
fur tipped with a
silvery sheen*

UNIQUE CHARACTERISTICS
The double-layered coat of
the Russian Shorthair is one
of a kind. It is so dense and
plush that the hair stands out
from the body, like seal fur.
The body is long, graceful, and
strong. Docile and quiet, these
cats are popular pets, particularly
in Sweden and New Zealand.

*Emerald-green
eyes*

ARCHANGEL CATS
Russian Shorthairs travelled on ships sailing
from the Russian port of Archangel (above) at
least as long ago as the 1800s. This gave them
their original name, Archangel Cats. For
unknown reasons, this breed has also been
known as the Spanish Cat and the Maltese Cat.

NEW COLOURS
The traditional Russian Shorthair is blue, a
colour that still predominates today. Recently,
breeders in Australia and New Zealand have
developed pure white and pure
black varieties, which are
becoming more
popular.

RUSSIAN
WHITE

*Large,
upright
ears of
thin skin*

*Delicately
boned legs with
small paws*

*White fur
appears almost
translucent*

SINGAPURA

THIS TINY BREED is a newcomer to the West, although it originated from the feral "drain cats of Singapore" that have lived in the streets of that Asian island for centuries. Developed in the U.S. in 1975, Singapuras are quite scarce, and their rarity means that they can fetch a very high price.

Eye colour changes at nine weeks

SINGAPURA KITTENS

Eyes and nose are outlined in black

TICKED FUR
Singapura fur is a warm ivory colour, ticked with dark seal brown. The tips of the hair are dark.

Sleek and silky fur feels like satin

SINGAPURA FACTS

• This breed's name is Malaysian for the island of Singapore.

• The feral ancestors of this breed are known for taking shelter in the drains of city streets.

• In 1988, an owner was offered $10,000 for his adult male Singapura.

SMALLEST CAT
This breed is the smallest in the world. A Singapura male often weighs under 2.7 kg (6 lb), compared to one of the largest cats, the Maine Coon, which weighs in at 8 kg (18 lb).

Large eyes and ears in proportion to the small head

FERAL CATS OF SOUTHEAST ASIA
Untamed cats living in the countries of
Southeast Asia have been used in recent years
to create new breeds, such as the Singapura
and the Wild Abyssinian. The feral cats
shown above are from Indonesia, which has
one of the world's largest cat populations.

SINGAPURA CHARACTERISTICS
The small, delicate body of this cat is
emphasized by its fine, close-lying coat.
Its ticked fur is described as "agouti"
because of its resemblance to the
South American rodent of that
name. These cats can be quite
bold. They enjoy the company
of people and often have
inquisitive natures.

SINGAPURA

Underparts are
paler than sides
of body

Tail is darker brown
than rest of body

BOMBAY

JET-BLACK FUR that shines like polished patent leather and vivid gold or copper eyes set the Bombay apart. The breed arose in 1958 when a pure black American Shorthair and a sable Burmese were crossed with the aim of creating a cat that looked similar to a miniature black panther.

BOMBAY

Wedge face with short muzzle

Eyes are blue at birth, then turn grey before finally changing to copper or gold

BOMBAY MARKET
This breed is named after the busy, colourful city of Bombay. This city is the cat's namesake because it is located in India, where black panthers are found.

OUTGOING PERSONALITY
An incredibly affectionate breed, the Bombay makes an ideal family pet. It has an assertive nature and is not easily intimidated by dogs. These cats are also vocal and virtually never stop purring. Bombays crave attention and hate to be left alone.

WILD LOOK-ALIKE

The wild cats that inspired the Bombay are actually leopards with a genetic mutation for black fur. Black panthers live mainly in forests, where their dark colour provides good camouflage.

BLACK PANTHER

SELF FUR COLOUR

The Bombay is an example of a self, or solid, coloured cat. This means that the fur is a single colour from root to tip. The depth of colour along the length of each individual hair does not vary. Typical self colours are black, white, red, and chocolate, or lighter shades of these, like blue, cream, and lilac.

SELF FUR

All Bombays are black – there are no other colour varieties.

Gleaming fur is short and dense

Medium-sized body is firm and muscular

Medium-length tail

WILD ABYSSINIAN

NEW TYPES OF CAT are constantly being created by breeders eager to bring more variety to domestic breeds. The Wild Abyssinian (no relation to the ordinary Abyssinian) was developed from feral cats in Singapore out of a desire to create a new breed with ticked fur.

WILD
ABYSSINIANS

"Necklaces" of
black fur
encircle neck

ASIAN ROOTS
There are conflicting theories about the origins of ticked tabbies. Some may have developed in Africa. However, new genetic studies suggest that ticked cats first appeared near India, and were carried east along spice routes, possibly in trading dhows (ships).

NEW BREED
The Wild Abyssinian was created in the 1980s. To maintain this breed's wild appearance, similar-looking feral cats have been imported to breed with pure Wild Abyssinians every five generations. This avoids the problems of inbreeding.

Oval paws are
large and
strong

Ticked fur is most
obvious on sides
and back

"M"-shaped marking on forehead imitates scarab shape

AFRICAN SCARAB BEETLE

SCARAB MARKINGS
Like other tabby cats, this breed has a dark, beetle-shaped pattern on the forehead. The ancient Egyptians believed the scarab was sacred, and its shape recurs in much of their art.

Head is long, with large eyes

WILD TABBY
The Wild Abyssinian is distinguished by the dark markings on its coat. The fur is golden brown ticked with black, with a ruddy orange undercoat. The tail is ringed with black stripes.

WILD ABYSSINIAN FACTS

• Despite their name, wild cats have not been used in the breeding of these cats.

• Wild Abyssinians have independent but friendly natures.

• Cats of this breed differ from ordinary Abyssinians in that they are larger and have tabby markings.

Well-defined tabby barring on legs

NON-PEDIGREE

THE POPULARITY of these cats has been unchallenged since their domestication 5,000 years ago. Today, over 95 per cent of the world's feline pets are non-pedigrees. These adaptable cats are as diverse as they are numerous. Each one has a unique appearance and personality.

Non-pedigree cats have highly individual markings.

BROWN TABBY

COMMON CATS
In many parts of the world, cats have featured in literature and art through the ages. One example is the famous Cheshire cat from Lewis Carroll's *Alice's Adventures in Wonderland* (1865). The grinning cat completely disappears except for his smile.

HUGE VARIETY
Most non-pedigree cats have tabby markings, a legacy from their wild relatives. Bi-coloured mixes are also common. Non-pedigree cats with coats of one pure colour are much rarer.

White hairs intermingled with black

White patches are random

ROBUST CITY PETS
Ordinary non-pedigrees are the most commonly kept cats in the world, partly because they are hardy and easy to care for. Black and white cats make ideal city pets because they have unshakeable temperaments.

Sturdy body shape

BLACK AND WHITE

Small, widely-spaced ears

Non-pedigree tom cats often have prominent jowls.

Broad tail with rounded tip has tabby markings along its length

TERRITORIAL TOMS
Both male and female cats patrol their territories, but tom cats lay claim to a much wider area. Male cats mark their part of the neighbourhood by spraying urine, leaving scratch marks, or rubbing their scent onto objects. They will fight to protect their territory.

Muscular, compact body

RED AND WHITE TABBY

The gene for red fur is likely to have originated in Asia.

Short legs, ending in powerful paws

NON-PEDIGREE FACTS
• The lifespan of a non-pedigree cat is normally longer than that of a pure-bred cat.

• The oldest recorded domestic cat was a British tabby who lived to the age of 36 years.

• Strangely, a cat's coat colour seems to reflect its temperament. Tabbies are generally placid and calm.

THE WORLD'S WILD CATS

ABOUT WILD CATS

THESE SHY AND MAINLY SOLITARY animals are highly sophisticated hunters. Most use the darkness of night to conceal themselves as they stalk their prey. Wild cats have been resilient and adaptable, successfully exploiting most of the world's habitats. However, many of these graceful creatures have become endangered because of hunting and habitat destruction.

SOFT AND STRIKING FUR
The ocelot is found in forests and scrubland from the southwestern U.S.A. to the tip of South America. However, today it is quite rare. Like many other strikingly patterned cats, it has been heavily hunted for its beautiful fur coat.

The ocelot stands about 45 cm (18 in) at the shoulder.

OCELOT

WILD CATS' HABITATS
The world's cats have adapted to live wherever they can find prey, from scorching deserts to icy uplands. This Siberian tiger from central Asia hunts throughout the winter. The largest of cats, it roams over a vast area in search of prey.

REARING YOUNG

A female wild cat must find a quiet, secluded place to give birth to her cubs. In their first months she must provide their food, as well as teach them to hunt for themselves. Like all wild cat young, these cheetah cubs face many hazards in their early years.

Long body with cloud-like markings

CAMOUFLAGED COAT

A cat's coat is designed to disguise the cat as it steals up on prey. Spots and stripes break up the outline of the cat's body, helping it blend into its habitat.

Many cats have a dark stripe running out from the eye.

CLOUDED LEOPARD

About the size of a small leopard, but it is not closely related

Long tail helps cat to balance

The rare clouded leopard is found in the forests of Southeast Asia.

WILD CAT FACTS

• Large wild cats are defined as roaring cats and small species as purring cats.

• Discovered in 1988, the Tshushima cat is found only on an island that lies between Japan and South Korea.

SMALL WILD CATS

THE SMALL WILD CATS are less well known than their larger relatives, but are far more numerous. The 28 species range from the tiny black-footed cat of southern Africa to the large puma. Many live in forests, where their striking, spotted patterns help them blend into the dappled shade.

ASIAN GOLDEN CAT

Golden cats have been known to be tamed.

ASIAN GOLDEN CAT

These cats are found in tropical forests in Nepal and Southeast Asia. Like most small cats, they are expert climbers and can catch birds in the treetops. Elusive and shy, Asian golden cats are rarely seen in the wild. They have become scarce as their habitat is destroyed by logging and farming.

FISHING CAT

These unusual Asian cats live close to water, where they grab fish, clams, snails, and other water-dwelling creatures from the shallows. Their front toes are webbed, which enables them to scoop prey out of the water. Their webbed paws also help them swim to hunt for fish.

THE WILD CAT
Varieties of the wild cat are found in Africa, Asia, and Europe. This Scottish wild cat may look like a domestic tabby, but it is a fierce hunter of rodents and birds. Wild cats in Europe generally live only in very remote areas. The African wild cat, the ancestor of all today's domestic breeds, is not as shy and can be found living close to human settlements.

Geoffroy's cat is about the same size as a domestic cat.

SAND CAT
Dense mats of fur protect these cats' feet from the searing hot Saharan sand. They will burrow underground, then wait until nightfall to emerge to hunt.

The sand cat weighs only 2.3 kg (5 lb).

GEOFFROY'S CAT
This high-altitude species is known in the southern part of South America where it lives as "the mountain cat". It has a short, broad head and can run, swim, and climb with ease. Geoffroy's cat may sleep in holes in trees during the day.

Fur keeps cat warm and provides camouflage

SERVAL AND CARACAL

THE GRASSLANDS and semi-deserts of Africa are home to these two medium-sized species. The caracal also ranges across the Middle East and Asia. Servals and caracals are formidable hunters, using their large ears to pinpoint small animals foraging in the grass.

SERVAL

SERVALS AND PEOPLE
Servals have long been hunted in Africa for food or for their skins, which are made into fur cloaks called *karrosses*. In East Africa, these cats are also sometimes kept as pets.

Each cat's pattern is different.

Pure black servals sometimes occur, particularly in Kenya.

SAVANNAH CAT
The serval stands about 61 cm (24 in) tall at the shoulder. It lives alone, usually near water, and employs its superb hearing and vision to track down its prey, often at dusk.

Like other small cats, servals cannot roar, but they do purr occasionally.

Very long front legs help these cats make quick escapes from hunting dogs.

Short tail

DESERT DEN
Open, arid country is the caracal's hunting ground. This cat is sometimes called the desert lynx, although it does not live in true deserts, nor is it a lynx. The female caracal makes her den in burrows or rocky caves, where she gives birth to up to four young. Caracals are now quite scarce.

NOCTURNAL HUNTER
Although caracals can kill animals much larger than themselves, they normally eat lizards, birds, small mammals, and even insects. They are very stealthy, keeping quiet so they can hear tiny movements as they stalk after nightfall.

The name comes from the Turkish "karakal", which means "black ears".

CARACAL

Fur tufts on ears can be 4.5 cm (1.75 in) long

INDIAN PAINTING OF A CARACAL AND TRAINER

Caracal in bird-catching competition

Caracals can make a barking noise.

TRAINED BIRD CATCHER
The caracal is known for its prowess at catching birds. It uses its paws to knock the birds to the ground as they take flight. For centuries, people in India have trained caracals for this skill.

CHEETAH

CHEETAH

THE SWIFTEST MAMMAL in the world, the cheetah outshines all other hunters when it comes to chasing down fast prey. These cats were once trained as hunting animals. During the 1600s, the Mughal emperor in India kept 1,000 cheetahs. His collection included a very rare white cheetah with bluish spots.

DANGEROUS DECLINE
Cheetahs almost became extinct during the last ice age. Only a tiny number survived. Since then, inbreeding over generations has caused a serious decline in the fertility of some males. Cheetahs are further threatened by poachers.

Flexible back

Long, slender legs

WATCHFUL MOTHER
The female cheetah is solitary, looking after her two to four cubs on her own. She will feed and protectively guard her young until they are 15 months old.

KING CHEETAH

Lives mainly in southern Africa

Dark markings form stripes instead of spots

These sleek cats live in the grasslands of Africa.

Skull is small, but longer than in other cats

Distinctive lines run down face from the eyes

RARE STRIPED MARKINGS
A cheetah with this unusual and very rare coat pattern was first reported in 1927. Although once mistakenly thought to be a separate species, the king cheetah occurs in litters along with normal, spotted cheetahs.

Golden coat with black spots camouflages the cat as it hunts during the day

Claws extended permanently to dig in when running

CHEETAH

SPRINTING CAT
Because it specializes in running, the cheetah is placed in a different genus from other cats. A cheetah can reach a maximum speed of 87 km/h (54 mph) over a short distance.

JAGUAR AND LEOPARD

JAGUAR

THESE TWO BOLDLY MARKED cats are often mistaken for each other. Leopards live in Africa and Asia, and they are agile, expert climbers. Jaguars are American cats with large, stocky bodies. They swim much better than they climb.

Large, ringed spots shaped like rosettes

SOUTH AMERICAN CAT
Jaguars now live mainly in the tropical forests of Central and South America. They are the largest cats on the American continents and were respected and admired by the Aztecs and Incas.

DARK CAMOUFLAGE
The black panther is simply a black-coloured leopard that lives in the dense, shadowy forests of Asia. It shares all the characteristics of its spotted counterpart.

Faint spotted pattern is visible on coat

BLACK PANTHER

KILLED FOR THEIR FUR
Although trade in jaguar skins is illegal, these pelts are proof that hunting continues. Hundreds of jaguars and leopards have been killed in recent years.

SWIMMING HUNTER
Jaguars swim well and often hunt in water, catching turtles, caimans, and fish. When the river level is low, these cats may even swim out to exposed sand banks and dig up turtles' nests for the eggs.

Perfectly balanced when climbing or resting

LEOPARD

There may be as many as 700,000 leopards in Africa.

OUNGING LEOPARD
hese superb climbers
ze around in trees after
hey have consumed their
ill. Here they are safe
nd can survey their
urroundings. Leopards in
ational parks tend to be
uch less wary than
heir unprotected kin.

Powerful paws help the leopard catch large prey like young giraffes.

PUMA, LYNX, AND BOBCAT

EQUALLY AT HOME on rocky mountain slopes or in semi-desert scrubland, these three adaptable cats can cope with hot, dry summers as well as cold, snowy winters. The puma and bobcat are found only in the Americas, while the lynx ranges over North America, Europe, and Asia. The closely related lynx and bobcat are distinguished from other cats by their unusual short, stumpy tails.

BOBCAT

The bobcat is one of the most common American wild cats.

Long side whiskers

Long legs

NORTH AMERICAN CAT
The bobcat's range stretches from Canada to Mexico. It is smaller than the lynx and its fur is more coarse, so its pelt is not considered as valuable. The bobcat occasionally strays into the suburbs of cities to catch rats and other small prey.

MOUNTAIN HUNTER
Pumas have strength and stamina. These cats will search huge distances for their prey. They may drag their catch 400 m (1,300 ft) from the site of the kill, to hide the carcass from scavengers.

Sandy brown coat is perfect for high plains camouflage

ENDANGERED EUROPEAN
The Spanish lynx is much smaller than the Eurasian lynx. It usually hunts rabbits, birds, and fish, but can also take young deer. These cats are extremely endangered – southern Spain is their last major stronghold.

Heavily spotted coat

SPANISH LYNX

TRAPPING FOR FUR
In winter, a lynx's coat is soft and thick, making these cats long sought after by trappers. Today, trapping is regulated. The North American lynx population varies mainly with the rise and fall in the number of its main prey, the snowshoe hare.

PURRING PUMA
The puma (its name is derived from an Inca word) is also known as the cougar or mountain lion. It is now found mainly in South America and the western U.S. Florida also has a tiny population. Road accidents are the major hazard for the 30–50 pumas left in Florida.

The pupils are round, like in the larger cats.

PUMA

LION

THESE MAJESTIC CATS once roamed from the southern tip of Africa to the Mediterranean and east through Asia. The Romans used to capture lions to fight gladiators in their arenas. Since then, the lions' range has dwindled to scattered areas of Africa and a small forest in India.

FEARSOME KILLER
Although lions rarely prey on people, this panel from the 8th century B.C. shows that it sometimes occurs. In recent times, lions killed 30 workers during the building of a railway in East Africa.

PROUD PAIR
Lions live in open country. The females do most of the hunting, co-operating to chase down prey. The male's job is to defend the pride's territory from other lions. His tremendous roar can be heard up to 8 km (5 miles) away.

FAMILY LIFE
Lions are the only cats that live in groups. The pride may have about 12 members, most of them related females and their cubs. When the young males reach adulthood they must either leave or fight the dominant male.

Massive mane can intimidate rivals

Male lion marks territory by spraying his urine on trees and shrubs

ASIATIC LIONS
At the beginning of the century, there were less than a dozen lions left in Asia. Today, under strict protection in the Gir Forest of India, their numbers have risen to over 250.

AFRICAN LION
AND LIONESS

Coat lacks markings

Tail, especially the tuft, is used to communicate with other lions

TIGER

THIS LARGEST MEMBER of the cat family is potentially the most ferocious. The tiger must claim a large territory in order to catch the food it needs to survive. This often brings these cats into conflict with humans. Today, there may be fewer than 5,000 tigers left in the wild.

WHITE TIGER
This stunning colour variety is a natural but rare occurrence in tigers from central India. Over 100 white tigers have been bred in zoos. One sighting of a tiger without stripes has also been recorded.

INDIAN TIGER

Southern Asian tigers are smaller and have brighter coats than northern tigers.

Low-slung, strong body

TIGERS AND PEOPLE
Tiger-hunting has a long history. Elephants were once used in these hunts because they gave a relatively safe vantage point for the hunter.

INDIAN PAINTING OF A TIGER HUNT

SOLITARY NIGHTTIME PROWLER
Tigers live alone in dense forests across Asia, where they normally stay hidden. Unlike most cats, tigers like water and spend a great deal of time swimming or just keeping cool.

GREAT CAT OF ASIA

There are about seven subspecies of tiger, all of which are endangered. These different forms vary in size and colour. The Siberian tiger is the largest and rarest, weighing up to 384 kg (845 lb). It can jump 12 m (40 ft) – over four times its body length.

White areas of fur on head

Hair on cheeks is longer than rest of coat, particularly in older males

Razor-sharp canine teeth

TIGER FACTS

• The most notorious "man-eating" tiger was the Champawat tigress. She killed 436 people.

• Tigers rarely attack from the front, so Indian farmers wear face masks on the back of their heads to confuse the cats.

SIBERIAN TIGER

REFERENCE
SECTION

CAT CLASSIFICATION

CLASSIFICATION IS a scientific system that arranges living things into groups according to features they share. The class of mammals encompasses more than 4,000 species of warm-blooded animals with hair. Within this class there are 20 different orders, one of which, the meat-eating carnivores, includes cats, dogs, and bears. The cat family, Felidae, is divided into three main genera, which include some 39 distinct cat species.

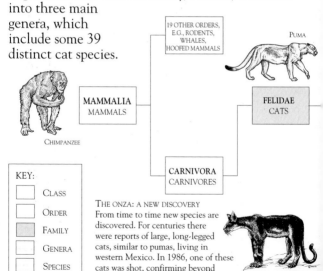

PUMA

19 OTHER ORDERS, E.G., RODENTS, WHALES, HOOFED MAMMALS

MAMMALIA
MAMMALS

FELIDAE
CATS

CHIMPANZEE

CARNIVORA
CARNIVORES

KEY:
- ☐ CLASS
- ☐ ORDER
- ☐ FAMILY
- ☐ GENERA
- ☐ SPECIES

THE ONZA: A NEW DISCOVERY
From time to time new species are discovered. For centuries there were reports of large, long-legged cats, similar to pumas, living in western Mexico. In 1986, one of these cats was shot, confirming beyond doubt the existence of the onza.

ONZA

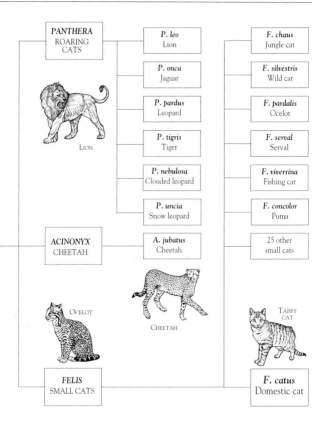

PANTHERA ROARING CATS	**P. leo** Lion	**F. chaus** Jungle cat
	P. onca Jaguar	**F. silvestris** Wild cat
	P. pardus Leopard	**F. pardalis** Ocelot
	P. tigris Tiger	**F. serval** Serval
	P. nebulosa Clouded leopard	**F. viverrina** Fishing cat
	P. uncia Snow leopard	**F. concolor** Puma
ACINONYX CHEETAH	**A. jubatus** Cheetah	25 other small cats
FELIS SMALL CATS		**F. catus** Domestic cat

LION

OCELOT

CHEETAH

TABBY CAT

ENDANGERED CATS

WILD CATS are under more threat today than ever before. Each year, many cats are killed for their attractive fur. In some places, the big cats are killed because their ground-up bones are superstitiously believed to cure ill health. Those cats that survive face shrinking habitats as cities, farms, and roads encroach into wild areas. Development has become the biggest threat to the survival of many cats.

EXAMPLE	HABITAT	REASONS FOR DECLINE
TIGER	Scattered areas of forest reserves, mainly in India, Southeast Asia, China, and as far north as Siberia.	The tiger is heavily hunted for its bones, which are ground up to make medicines. It is also killed because of its threat to people and livestock. There may be fewer than 5,000 in the wild.
MARGAY	Wooded forests from Mexico southwards to Argentina, east of the Andes Mountains.	Until the 1980s, huge numbers of margays were hunted for their pelts. Their numbers have fallen dramatically in the southern part of their range. Forest clearance now poses another serious threat.
SNOW LEOPARD	Remote mountainous areas of central Asia and India, usually at very high altitude.	As tigers grow scarce, snow leopards are hunted to make remedies from their bones. They are also killed because they prey on livestock. There may be only 5,400 snow leopards left.

EXAMPLE	HABITAT	REASONS FOR DECLINE
IRIOMOTE CAT	Ranges from the mountains down to the beaches of Iriomote Island, a Pacific island east of Taiwan.	Discovered in 1967, this cat lives only on the small Japanese island of Iriomote. Although it is now protected by law, hunting and habitat destruction have decreased its numbers to 100.
ASIATIC LION	Confined to the scrub and thorn forests of the Gir Forest National Park in Gujarat, west-central India.	Once found all over Asia, the Asiatic lion was hunted almost to extinction in the early 1900s. Their numbers fell to 12, but have risen to 250 since their protection in the Gir reserve.
SCOTTISH WILD CAT	Mountainous, forested Highlands area in the central and northern parts of Scotland.	Hunting began the Scottish wild cat's decline, but these cats are now protected. Today their greatest threat is interbreeding with domestic cats, which produces hybrid wild cats.
CLOUDED LEOPARD	Densely forested areas of Southeast Asia, mainly in Java, Sumatra, Borneo, and Taiwan.	Destruction of their forest habitats is the major threat to these cats. They are also hunted for their striking, marbled fur. Pesticides, used in farming, may also be poisoning some cats.
SPANISH LYNX	Ranges from remote mountains to coastal areas in southwest Spain and neighbouring parts of Portugal.	The decline of this species is mainly due to hunting, but also to its shrinking habitat. Lynxes are still trapped, and some are killed on roads. Their numbers are now fewer than 400.

CHOOSING A CAT

A CAT MAY LIVE for more than 15 years, and it needs a caring home for life. Once you have decided to make this commitment, you must choose the right companion. You may want to adopt an older cat, as kittens demand a lot of attention. However, kittens adapt easily to a new home.

Should show no evidence of pain when handled

THE HEALTHY KITTEN

A young kitten should not be taken from its mother before it is three months old. A healthy kitten is lively, playful, and alert, although it may sleep for long periods.

Body should be plump, but a pot-belly may be a sign of roundworms.

SEXING A KITTEN

The anus and penis in a male cat are farther apart than the anus and vulva in a female.

Anus

Vulva

Testes

Penis

FEMALE   MALE

You may want to have your kitten neutered when it reaches four to six months of age.

Legs should show no signs of lameness

WHAT YOU SHOULD LOOK FOR

THE EARS
Check that the earflaps are not torn or bitten. Look inside the ears for excess wax or other discharge. A bad odour could indicate infection.

THE EYES
These should be clean, clear, and bright, with no signs of discharge. The inner eyelid (a white film) in the corner of the eye should not be visible.

THE NOSE
Make sure the nose is cool and damp. A runny or scabby nose is usually a sign of illness. Yellowish discharge suggests some sort of infection.

MOUTH AND GUMS
Carefully open the mouth to check that the teeth are not broken. The gums and tongue should be pink and healthy. The breath should be fresh.

THE COAT
Look for a clean, glossy coat. Dark specks are evidence of fleas. Any hair loss, particularly bald patches, could be an indication of ringworm.

THE REAR
Any stains on the rear are likely to mean the kitten has a digestive disorder. If you see what looks like small grains of rice, the kitten has tapeworms.

CARING FOR YOUR CAT

FOR THE MOST PART, cats can take care of themselves. However, they have certain basic needs, as well as individual demands, that you should be prepared for. Even the most independent cats sometimes need special care.

CAT CARRIER

WHAT YOU MIGHT NEED
A basic range of equipment is shown here. An indoor cat is likely to require more equipment than a cat that can go outside.

FOOD AND WATER BOWL

ELASTICATED COLLAR

NAIL CLIPPERS

RUBBER BRUSH

TOYS

CAT BED

METAL COMB

LITTER TRAY AND SCOOP

BRISTLE BRUSH

SCRATCHING PAD

FEEDING (FEED CAT AT THE SAME TIME AND PLACE AT LEAST TWICE A DAY)

Type	Preparation	Value	Comments
Canned food (includes meat or fish, and cereal).	Serve straight from can into clean bowl.	Cats find this the tastiest type of prepared cat food.	Must be fresh; spoils quickly in hot weather.
Semi-moist (includes soya, processed meat, and often sugar).	Open foil pack and serve into clean bowl.	Cats prefer softer texture to most dry cat foods.	The drier the food, the more water the cat needs to drink.
Dry food (includes dried, processed meat, and cereal).	Pour from box or packet into bowl.	Hard texture prevents tartar from forming on teeth and gums.	Lightest to carry and does not spoil easily.
Milk (either cow's milk or special milk for cats).	Pour from carton into clean bowl.	Valuable source of vitamins, calcium, and other minerals.	Cow's milk may cause diarrhoea in some cats.
Fresh foods (egg, fish, meat, poultry, or cheese).	Should always be fresh. Cook before feeding to your cat.	Adds variety and interest to cat's diet. Good for convalescing cats.	These foods are not nutritionally balanced on their own.

GROOMING YOUR CAT

Grooming helps eliminate the problems of loose hairs around the home, furballs, and fleas. As you are combing the fur you may see dark specks; these indicate that fleas are present. Groom your cat outdoors with a special fine-toothed comb to locate the fleas. Special flea sprays, powders, or collars can then be used to treat the cat.

Tangles can be removed with a metal comb.

COMMON HEALTH PROBLEMS

CATS ARE NORMALLY healthy, but they can be afflicted by various ailments. Most of a cat's illnesses can be prevented by vaccinations and check-ups at the vet. You can purchase veterinary insurance to cover your pet. In case of serious emergencies, contact a vet immediately.

INJURED CAT

ACCIDENTS ON THE ROAD

It is impossible to prevent a cat from crossing roads. Night is the most dangerous time, when a cat can be blinded by car headlights. If possible, keep your cat indoors after dark.

• If a cat has been hit by a car, carefully lift it out of danger. You must keep its body flat in case of internal injury. Place your hands under the cat's chest and pelvis, or use a sheet like a stretcher. Do not raise the cat's head.

• After an accident, a vet should always be called, since it is difficult to assess internal injuries. Make sure that the cat is kept warm and still.

DIGESTIVE PROBLEMS

There are many reasons for digestive upsets. Symptoms might include vomiting, loss of appetite or weight loss, diarrhoea, or constipation.

• It is normal for cats to vomit occasionally, for example, if they have eaten grass. If vomiting occurs with diarrhoea, or if any blood is present in the stools, contact a vet immediately.

• Watch out for the appearance of the third eyelid, or swelling or tenderness in the cat's abdomen. If any symptoms persist for more than 24 hours, a vet should be called.

• In cases of constipation, give your cat a teaspoonful of liquid paraffin in its food once a day for several days.

POISONING

Some medicines, such as aspirin, are fatal for cats. Household chemicals are also poisonous and should be stored safely away from your pets. Symptoms of poisoning include vomiting, convulsions, drooling, or collapse.

• Cats will drink car anti-freeze even though it is highly toxic. In this case, rush the cat to the vet, who may be

able to provide an antidote to block the effect of the poison.

• A cat's coat can become contaminated, and when it tries to clean itself the cat can be poisoned. If possible, wash the cat and wrap it in a towel so it cannot lick its fur. In severe cases, contact the vet.

WOUNDS AND BLEEDING

Cats may receive wounds in fights or be injured in other ways. If the cat is not in too much distress you should be able to attend to the wounds. Consult a vet if the injuries seem serious.

• In cases of severe bleeding, apply pressure on the wound with absorbent cotton wool and wrap a bandage around it to keep it in place.

• Any bites or punctures should be carefully cleaned. Clip the fur around the wound and wash the area in warm salt water.

• An abscess may develop, which should burst after 24 hours if bathed frequently. Keep cleaning the wound. Antibiotics may be necessary.

PARASITES

A range of parasites, both internal and external, can infest cats. Fleas are the most common affliction. Kittens and cats that hunt a lot are most susceptible to internal parasites.

• Keep a close watch for fleas, ticks, and other pests in your cat's coat. You can treat your pet with sprays or powders. Clean the areas of your

home, such as carpets and the cat's bedding, where fleas tend to breed.

• Typical symptoms of worms include weight loss, diarrhoea, a pot-bellied appearance, or the cat excessively licking its behind. Your vet can prescribe tablets or deworming paste to treat the problem.

FIRST AID

SOME COMMON EMERGENCIES can be handled at home when your cat gets into trouble. However, if you suspect your cat needs further assistance, contact a vet without delay. It is useful to have a few first aid supplies at home for emergencies.

A BASIC FIRST AID KIT
1 Safe disinfectant. 2 Human eye wash.
3 Liquid paraffin (for cat constipation).
4 Antiseptic cream. 5 Antiseptic wash.
6 Round-ended scissors. 7 Bandages.
8 Rectal thermometer. 9 Tweezers.
10 Lint gauze. 11 Adhesive dressing.
12 Cotton wool. 13 Cotton buds.

TAKING A CAT'S TEMPERATURE
First, gently restrain the cat – otherwise it may bite and scratch. Lift the tail and insert a lubricated thermometer about 2.5 cm (1 in) into the anus. Hold it there for at least one minute. The temperature should be about 38.6°C (100°F).

Hold scruff of neck

Try concealing the tablet in food.

GIVING TABLETS
Open the cat's mouth, tip its head back, and place the tablet as far back in the throat as possible. Then hold the mouth closed, stroking the throat until the cat swallows.

REMOVING FOREIGN BODIES
If splinters or other objects become stuck between your cat's toes you can remove them using tweezers. Ask a vet to remove anything embedded in the pad since this will be painful for the cat and may cause bleeding.

Use tweezers

Hold firmly

REMOVING FOREIGN BODY

DISINFECTING WOUND

Damp cotton wool

TREATING THE EYES
If your cat has an eye infection, gently wipe away discharge. Then carefully apply eye drops or ointment and hold the eyes closed for a few seconds.

BANDAGING MINOR WOUNDS
In case of a wound, first use pressure to stop the bleeding. Then clean the area and attach a gauze pad by wrapping a bandage around it (not too tightly!).

CHECKING VITAL SIGNS
If a cat is unconscious, call a vet immediately. Check for breathing and pulse. Feel for the heartbeat below the cat's elbow on the lower part of its chest. If necessary, stimulate the heart by pressing gently.

Watch for breathing

CHECKING BREATHING

Heart rate should be 160–240 beats per minute

Cat must be on right side

CHECKING HEARTBEAT

UNDERSTANDING YOUR CAT

CATS COMMUNICATE vocally by purring, miaowing, or hissing. They also express themselves with facial and body language. Domestic cats share much of their behaviour with their wild cousins. Yet they have had to adapt to share their territories with other animals and people.

CLAIMING POSSESSION

When a cat rubs against objects it is marking its territory. Every cat has scent glands around its chin and near the rear of its body. Your cat may rub against your legs to claim you as its own.

PURRING IN CONTENTMENT

No one is certain how a cat makes its characteristic purring sound. It may be produced by vibrating membranes near the vocal cords in the throat. Purring normally indicates that a cat is relaxed and content; however, an ill or upset cat may also purr occasionally.

Ears perked up to collect information

Ears slightly forwards but relaxed

Eyes half-closed in pleasure

ALERT
Something has caught this cat's attention. Its eyes are opened wide as it stares intently at a potential threat or prey. The cat pauses, assessing the intrusion, but remains vigilant.

CONTENT
Relaxed and trouble-free, this cat is settling down to sleep in comfortable surroundings. Its eyes are half-closed and not focusing specifically on anything. The cat may be purring.

Ears flattened

Pupils dilated in fear

Eyes watchful

Tongue arched in anger

CURIOUS
The cat holds its ears forwards to pick up sounds as it assesses the object of its curiosity. Its body language will show uncertainty (the tail may be flicking), which can easily switch to aggression.

AGGRESSIVE
To show extreme fear or anger, a cat flattens its ears and opens its mouth to bare its sharp teeth. The whiskers are held out, and the cat hisses fiercely to intimidate its enemy.

AMAZING CAT RECORDS

THERE IS NO SHORTAGE of remarkable facts about cats.
Many of these arise from their long and colourful
association with people. Cats also have many unique
adaptations that have evolved over time.

SIZE

• Largest wild cat :
Siberian tiger – up to
4 m (13 ft) from nose
to tip of tail; can weigh
up to 384 kg (845 lb).

• Smallest wild cat:
Black-footed cat –
57.5 cm (23 in) from
nose to tip of tail.

• Lightest wild cat:
Rusty-spotted cat –
weighs 1.36 kg (3 lb).

• Heaviest domestic
cat: A male tabby from
Australia weighed
21.3 kg (nearly 47 lb)
when he died in 1986.

• Lightest domestic
cat: A Siamese cross
weighed .79 kg (1 lb
12 oz) at two years old.

HISTORY

• Largest burial:
300,000 mummified
cats were found in one
ancient Egyptian tomb.

• Earliest cats in war:
In 500 B.C., the Persians
used cats as a shield
against the Egyptians,
who dared not kill their
sacred animal.

• First cat liberation:
In 1000 A.D., a
Japanese decree freed
all house cats to catch
mice on farms.

• Most unusual use:
In Britain, in the
14th–18th centuries,
dead cats were built
into the walls of houses
to scare away mice.

UNUSUAL CATS

• Most unusual
mutation: Domestic
cats born with
wing-like flaps of skin
on their backs. One
Swedish cat had a
"wingspan" of 59 cm
(23 in).

• Most body parts: In
1975 in the U.S.A., a
domestic cat was born
with five legs, six paws,
and 30 toes.

• Most unique: The
one and only example
of a "litigon" – the
offspring of a lion and
a tigon (itself a cross
between a tiger and a
lioness) – was born in a
zoo in Calcutta, India.

HUNTING

• Best mouser: A tortoiseshell cat living in a whisky distillery in Scotland. She killed 28,899 mice – three a day for 20 years.

• Most ferocious: The record number of people killed by a single cat is 84 by a lion, 400 by a leopard, and 436 by a tiger.

FAME

• Most famous film star: Leo the MGM lion starred in many films and did stunts.

• Most famous fictional cats: The cat characters in T.S. Eliot's *Old Possum's Book of Practical Cats* (1939), on which the award-winning musical *Cats* is based.

FAMILY LIFE

• Best breeder: A tabby cat from Texas, U.S.A. gave birth to 420 kittens in her life.

• Oldest mother: In 1987, a non-pedigree cat had two kittens at the age of 30 years.

• Most hazardous: The male lion of the pride may kill any lion cubs that are not his own.

LIFESPAN

• Oldest domestic cat: A British tabby that lived to the age of 34. She died in 1957.

• Oldest wild cat: A lion in Cologne Zoo in Germany that lived to be 29 years old. Lions in the wild generally live for only about 12 years.

FEATS

• Farthest traveller: A U.S. Persian walked 2,400 km (1,500 miles) in 13 months to find her owner.

• Best climber: In 1950, a four-month-old kitten followed climbers to the top of the 4,478 m (14,691 ft) Matterhorn in the Alps.

MOST VALUABLE

• Most expensive meal: A Persian ate a diamond and ruby ring worth £3,200.

• Most valuable collection: A Texas farmer kept up to 1,400 cats on his farm.

• Most costly kittens: Bengal kittens may sell for over £1,000 each.

Resources

The main offices of cat organizations are listed here. These can refer you to your nearest branch. Please include a stamped, self-addressed envelope.

ORGANIZATIONS FOR CAT HEALTH

Blue Cross
1 Hugh Street
London SW1V 1QQ

British Association of Homoeopathic Veterinary Surgeons
Chinham House
Stanford-in-the-Vale
Faringdon
Oxfordshire SN7 8NQ

British Small Animal Veterinary Association
Kingsley House
Church Lane
Shurdington
Cheltenham
Gloucestershire
TL51 5TQ

Feline Advisory Bureau
235 Upper
Richmond Road
Putney
London SW15 6SN

People's Dispensary for Sick Animals (PDSA)
Whitechapel Way
Priorslee
Telford
Shropshire TF2 9PQ

SHOW BODIES

These organizations can supply up-to-date information on pedigree standards for cats, registration, and details about cat shows.

The Cat Association of Great Britain (CA)
Mill House
Letcombe Regis
Oxfordshire OX12 9JD

Federation Internationale Feline (FIFe)
Boerhaavelaan 23
NO-5644 BB Eindhoven
The Netherlands

The Governing Council of the Cat Fancy (GCCF)
4–6 Penel Orlieu
Bridgewater
Somerset TA6 3PG

ORGANIZATIONS AGAINST ANIMAL CRUELTY

The Cat Action Trust
P.O. Box 1639
London W8 4KY

Royal Society for the Prevention of Cruelty to Animals
The Causeway
Horsham
West Sussex RH12 1HG

OTHER USEFUL ORGANIZATIONS

The Cat's Protection League
17 Kings Road
Horsham
West Sussex RH13 5PP
(Provides educational material about domestic cats and assists the general welfare of cats)

Ministry of Agriculture, Fisheries, and Food
Hook Rise South
Tolworth
Surbiton, Surrey
(For advice on import and export laws and requirements for cats)

Society for Companion Animal Studies
7 Botanic Crescent Lane
Glasgow G20 8AA
(For information on
relationships between
pets and people)

Southern Aviaries
Tinkers Lane
Hadlow Down
Uckfield
East Sussex TN22 4EU
(Mail-order supplier of
equipment for cats)

Wood Green Animal Shelters
Kings Bush Farm
London Road
Godmanchester
Cambridgeshire PE18 8LJ
(Takes in strays and tries
to find homes for them)

ORGANIZATIONS INVOLVED WITH WILD CATS

These organizations have
information about the
world's wild cats.

Cat Survival Trust
Marlind Centre
Codicote Road
Welwyn
Hertfordshire AL6 9TV

International Society of Cryptozoology
P.O. Box 43070
Tucson, AZ 85733 U.S.A.
(For information on
unexplained cat sightings
worldwide)

IUCN/SSC Cat Specialist Group
World
Conservation Centre
Avenue du Mont-Blanc
1196 Gland
Switzerland

The Ridgeway Trust
P.O. Box 29
Hastings
East Sussex

The Tiger Trust
Chevington
Bury St. Edmunds
Suffolk
IP29 5RG

Worldwide Fund for Nature (WWF)
Panda House
Weyside Park
Godalming
Surrey GU7 1XR

Zoological Society of London
Regent's Park
London NW1 4RY

CAT MAGAZINES

All About Cats
40 Gray's Inn Road
London WC1X 8LR

BBC Wildlife
Broadcasting House
Whiteladies Road
Bristol BS8 2LR

Cat World
10 Western Road
Shoreham-by-Sea
West Sussex BN43 5WD

Cats
Our Dogs
Publishing Co. Ltd.
5 James Leigh Street
Manchester M1 6EX

Kennel and Cattery Management
P.O. Box 45
Dorking
Surrey RH5 512

Your Cat
EMAP Pursuit
Publishing Ltd.
Bretton Court
Bretton
Peterborough PE3 8DZ

Wild About Animals
40 Gray's Inn Road
London WC1X 8LR

Glossary

ADAPTATION
An evolutionary process by which living things adapt to their habitats.

AWN HAIR
Short, thick, bristly hair which lies underneath a cat's top coat.

BINOCULAR VISION
Using both eyes to focus on and judge the distance of an object.

BLOODLINE
The ancestors of a cat, stretching back over generations.

BREED
Cats that are similar to each other, based on a specific set of standards.

CAMOUFLAGE
Colours or markings that help animals blend into their surroundings.

CARNIVORE
An animal that eats the flesh of other animals.

CARPAL PADS
Anti-skid pads found on the "wrists" of the cat's front legs.

CATTERY
A place where cats are bred or can board.

CLASSIFICATION
A system of organizing living things into groups according to features they have in common.

COBBY
A compact, rounded body shape in cats.

CROSS-BREEDING
Mating between two different breeds.

DOMINANT CHARACTERISTIC
A genetic characteristic that occurs in both parent and offspring.

DOUBLE COAT
Short, soft undercoat with a thick, resilient outer coat.

DOWN HAIR
Short, soft hair that grows in tufts and provides insulation.

EVOLUTION
A theory that explains how living things adapt and change over generations.

EXTINCTION
When a species ceases to exist, either naturally or through human interference.

FELINE
Member of the cat family, Felidae.

FERAL
A once-domestic cat that has reverted to living in the wild.

FLEHMENING
The grimace a cat makes when it draws air over the Jacobsen's organ in its mouth.

GROOMING
Licking and wiping of the fur to keep it clean and spread the cat's scent around its body.

GUARD HAIR
Long, coarse hairs that make up the cat's top coat. These carry the pattern of the fur.

HABITAT
The environment in which an animal lives.

HYBRID
Offspring that results from the breeding of different species.

INBREEDING
Breeding between relatives, which can cause genetic mutations in the offspring.

JACOBSEN'S ORGAN
An organ in the roof of
a cat's mouth that is
linked with the senses
of smell and taste.

LITTER
All the kittens born to a
mother in a single birth.

MOULTING
The (usually) seasonal
shedding of the coat.

MUTATION
A genetic change that
can be either harmless
or unhealthy.

NEUTERING
Surgically removing the
means of reproduction.

NOCTURNAL
Active at night.

NON-PEDIGREE
A cat that has not been
specially bred to achieve
certain standards.

ON HEAT
The period in which a
female cat looks for a
partner to mate with.

PADS
Tough, leathery, furless
cushions on the
underside of a cat's feet.

PAPILLAE
The tiny, pointed hooks
on a cat's tongue that
give the tongue its
rough surface.

PARASITES
Animals, like fleas, that
live off other creatures.

PEDIGREE
The written record of the
line of descent of a
pure-bred cat.

POINTED
Fur pattern with darker
areas on the head, ears,
legs, paws, and tail.

POLYDACTYL
A cat born with more
toes than is normal.

PREDATOR
An animal that hunts to
catch the food it needs
to survive.

PRIDE
A group of lions, usually
closely related, that live
and hunt together.

QUEEN
Unneutered female cat.

RANGE
The area in which an
individual animal or a
species lives.

RETRACTABLE CLAWS
Claws that are sheathed
when a cat is relaxed,
and extended only
when necessary.

SELECTIVE BREEDING
Breeding of animals by
humans in order to
achieve desired features.

SPECIES
A group of similar
animals that can breed
together to produce
fertile young.

SPRAYING
When a cat (usually
male) sprays urine to
mark its territory.

TABBY
Dark coat markings that
can be stripes, blotches,
or spots.

TAPETUM LUCIDUM
Mirror-like layer of cells
behind the cat's retina.
These cells reflect light
for good night vision.

TERRITORY
Area that a particular
cat occupies and defends
against other cats.

THIRD EYELID
Membrane underneath
the outer eyelid that
only appears when the
cat is injured or ill.

TICKING
A fur colour
distinguished by bands
of colour on each hair.

TOM
Unneutered male cat.

WHISKERS
Specialized, stiff hairs
with highly sensitive
nerves at their roots.

Index

Acknowledgements

**Dorling Kindersley would
like to thank:**
Hilary Bird for the index.
Carlton Hibbert, Myfanwy Hancock, and
Kate Eagar for design assistance.
Caroline Potts and Robert Graham for
picture research assistance.

Photographs by:
Jane Burton, Steve Gorton,
Marc Henrie, Colin Keates,
Dave King, Tim Ridley, Jerry Young

Illustrations by:
Gill Ellsbury, Angelica Elsebach,
Chris Forsey, Craig Gosling (Indiana
University Medical Illustration
Department), Kenneth Lilly,
Stanley Cephas Johnson, Janos Marffy,
Malcolm McGregor, John Temperton,
Ann Winterbotham, John Woodcock,
Dan Wright

Picture credits: t = top b = bottom
c = centre l = left r = right
The publisher would like to thank the
following for their kind permission to
reproduce the photographs:

Adams Picture Library 109tr; Alaska State
Library/Early Prints, 01-2034 129tr; Alison
Ashford 92tr; Aquila/ M.W. Fowles 17tl,
M.C. Wilfes 81tl; Bridgeman Art
Library/British Museum 2cl, 130tl, 132br;
The British Library, Oriental and India
Office Collections 123 bl; Hilda
Blackmore 107bl; Chanan 88/89, 89tr,
100l; Paul Casey/CSCA 97tl; Bruce
Coleman 120l, 120cr, 123tl, 126bl, 131cr;
Mary Evans 56tl, 64tr, 73tl, 77cr, 106tl,
114cl; ET Archive 87tl; Robert Harding
Picture Library 58tr, 66tl, 94bl, 104tr,
Rainbird/Derrick Nitty 12l; Marc Henrie
63tl, 70tr, 75br, 103tl; Hulton Deutsch
Collection 88tl; Michael Holford 98l,
112tl; Image Bank/Joseph Van Os 97tr,
110tl, 119c, Guido Alberto Rossi 125tl;
Larry Johnson 48; John Massey-Stewart
107tr, Natural History Museum 3cl, 14,
15tl, 15b; Nature Photographers/Michael
Gore 42r, 43tl, 131tl; NHPA 125tr, Planet
Earth/Carol Farneti 27tr, 31tr, 127tl,
Jonathan Scott 35tr, 36tl, Anup and
Manoj Shah 33tr, 127cr; Pobjoy Mint Ltd
54tl; Tony Stone Images/Paul Chesley
69tr, Jeanne Drake 16tl, 118b, 119tr, Ian
Murphy 124/125, Mark Peterson 39b,
Manoj Shah 125br, 128bl, 133; Tonda M.
Straede 80l; World Pictures 105tr; Tetsu
Yamazaki 49, 51b, 55tr, 89tr, 94cr, 98br,
99r, 112r, 113l; Jerry Young front cover br,
10/11, 40/41b, 67tl; Zefa 25tr, 41t, 90tr, 121tr.

Every effort has been made to trace the
copyright holders and we apologise in
advance for any unintentional omissions.
We would be pleased to insert the
appropriate acknowledgement in any
subsequent edition of this publication.